Miku dé Nihongo
Sing with Hatsune Miku and Learn Japanese Culture & Conversations!

Noricco Toyoda

Japanese is my native and favorite language. I love the structure, the pronunciation the flexibility and the variation. I also love Hatsune Miku and her songs. She is a Japanese culture and sensation has become an entity with persona. Writing this book has been my great pleasure, listening, interpreting and translating her songs and it was so much fun to think of conversation skits for practice.

I hope you will enjoy singing Hatsune Miku while learning this language. It's not difficult; it's just different. By singing the songs repeatedly you will naturally learn the language while understanding the interpretation and the background culture. Enjoy it so your brain accepts it better! Happy cerebral stimulation is the secret of learning.

All of the songs come with explanation of the background culture or analysis of the lyrics for practical conversation skits in both casual and formal ways of speaking.
Try to talk as if you were with Hatsune Miku so that you will have fun learning the language. For some of the songs, VOCALO producers helped me to give you the true interpretation of the lyrics.
This book is for all the fans of Hatsune Miku, VOCALOID or those who love Japan or even for those who are thinking of learning Japanese or Japanese culture.

Acknowledgement

I would like to express my gratitude to all who supported and assisted me. Those from Crypton, VOCALO producers, the designers and the editors from Sanshusha and of course Miku herself and her colleague VOCALOID. I cannot thank my husband enough, who has been patiently supporting me in many ways. How can you be so nice to the author near the deadline!
In loving memory of my mother who is soon passing away to "Saihate",

Noricco A.Toyoda

►Contents

Preface ·· 2
What's Hatsune Miku? ································ 6
How to Use this Book ······························· 8
How to Use SONOCA ································ 12

1 ハロ／ハワユ (Haro Hawayu)

Lyrics ····································· 16
Context and Japanese Culture ············· 28
Let's try! Let's practice! Let's talk in Japanese! ·············· 30

2 デスクトップ・シンデレラ (Desktop Cinderella)

Lyrics ···································· 36
Context and Japanese Culture ············· 48
Let's try! Let's practice! Let's write in Japanese! ············· 50

3 春が来た (Haru ga kita)

Lyrics ···································· 56
Context and Japanese Culture ············· 62
Let's try! Let's practice! Let's talk in Japanese! ·············· 64

4 ハジメテノオト (Hajimete no oto)

Lyrics ···································· 70
Context and Japanese Culture ············· 82
Let's try! Let's practice! Let's talk in Japanese! ·············· 84

5 サイハテ (Saihate)

Lyrics ···································· 90
Context and Japanese Culture ············· 96
Let's try! Let's practice! Let's talk in Japanese! ·············· 98

6 Tell Your World

Lyrics	104
Context and Japanese Culture	110
Let's try! Let's practice! Let's talk in Japanese!	112

7 リモコン (Rimokon)

Lyrics	118
Context and Japanese Culture	130
Let's try! Let's practice! Let's talk in Japanese!	132

8 微風ドライブ (Soyokaze Drive)

Lyrics	138
Context and Japanese Culture	144
Let's try! Let's practice! Let's talk in Japanese!	146

9 桜ノ雨 (Sakura no ame)

Lyrics	152
Context and Japanese Culture	164
Let's try! Let's practice! Let's talk in Japanese!	166

10 巡り、夏 (Meguri, natsu)

Lyrics	172
Context and Japanese Culture	184
Let's try! Let's practice! Let's talk in Japanese!	186

Simple Grammar Rules & Pronunciation Guide for Japanese	190
Verb & Adjective Conjugation	192
50 Hiragana List	194
50 Katakana List	196
Author's Profile	198

▶What's Hatsune Miku?

Developed by Crypton Future Media, INC., Hatsune Miku is a software which anybody can make sing by entering lyrics and a melody. Many creators made music with Hatsune Miku and posted their creations to the Internet, sparking a worldwide movement. Hatsune Miku has also garnered attention as a character with an expansive merchandise lineup as well as live concerts, and her popularity continues to grow worldwide.

クリプトン・フューチャー・メディア株式会社が開発した、歌詞とメロディーを入力して誰でも歌を歌わせることができる「ソフトウェア」です。大勢のクリエイターが「初音ミク」で音楽を作り、インターネット上に投稿したことで一躍ムーブメントとなりました。「キャラクター」としても注目を集め、今ではバーチャル・シンガーとしてグッズ展開やライブを行うなど多方面で活躍するようになり、人気は世界に拡がっております。

Crypton Future Media, INC. is a music technology and licensing company based in Japan. Crypton started out as music software importer for Japan distribution, but engaged quickly in the development of voice synthesizer software.
Hatsune Miku is one of the six characters developed for the voice synthesizer product, and the character illustration is featured on the software package. By incorporating stylized illustrations for each character, Crypton encapsulated a fundamental element of contemporary Japanese pop-culture while connecting it to music and creativity.

piapro.net

　クリプトン・フューチャー・メディア株式会社は、音楽技術とライセンス事業を扱う日本企業です。クリプトン社は、音楽ソフトウェアの日本への輸入販売業から始まり、その後まもなく音声合成ソフトウェアの開発に携わりました。初音ミクは、音声合成ソフトとして開発された6人のキャラクターの一人であり、そのキャラクターのイラストはソフトウェアのパッケージに表されています。
　それぞれのキャラクターにイラストを関連付けることで、クリプトン社は、現代の日本のポップカルチャーの基本的な要素を込め、それを音楽と創造に結びつけました。

▶How to Use This Book

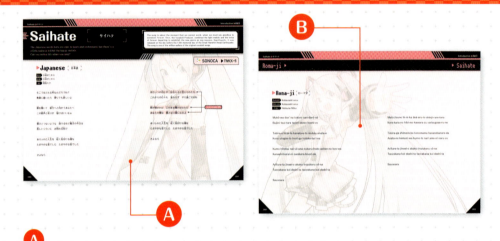

A

Original lyrics in Japanese. Each Kanji character has pronunciation guides in Hiragana on the top.

The brief introduction to the song will be found on the top near the title: what kind of melody on the top left and the history or information about the song on the top right to assist you to understand the song better before studying.

B

The song is written in the alphabet ("Roma-ji") to help you to pronounce Japanese words when you sing. The Roma-ji system in this book is slightly different from the official Roma-ji writing system in some ways to assist pronunciation.

[The Roma-ji system in this book]

	function	example	explanation
①	dash "-" to indicate particles	hajimete-no	"no" is a particle
②	separated double vowels	a'u	not like /oo/ in auto, but /awoo/
③	long vowel	â	pronounce to prolong the vowel /a:/
④	é	/dé/	/dE/like Denmark

C

English translation of the lyrics. Songs were translated to help language learning by giving the meaning of the words and phrases instead of the poetic images or rhyming.

As for English translation except for "Tell Your World", the songs were translated to give the meaning of the words, rather than poetic images.

D

Quoting phrases which symbolize Japanese culture or the keys of the lyrics. The following marks indicate the languages and meaning.

=Nihongo
=Rôma-ji
=English
=Meaning

E

Enjoy the song and learn Japanese culture while reading "Tips" which contain interesting information such as background culture, Keywords, interesting facts about the song.

009

How to Use This Book

F

We picked up basic structures of Japanese language from the lyrics and give a grammatical analysis. (In some units, you might find greetings or writing). We've explained the grammar as simply as possible, but could not avoid the following grammatical words.

[Grammatical terms]

terms	function	example
V	Verb	iku
Noun	A word (other than a pronoun) used to identify any of a class of people, places, or things (common noun), or to name a particular one of these (proper noun).	uta
Adj	Adjective: a word that describes or clarifies a noun, such as sweet, cute, beautiful.	Kawaii
Particle	See below.	
honorific	adding politeness to a Verb	-desu -masu
denial	adding denial meaning	-nai
conjunctive	making a verb connective form	-te

particle(s) follows nouns, verbs and adjectives to indicate its roles.

particle: subject	article which indicates the noun is the subject.	<particle: subject "ga">	watashi-ga	I
particle: object	particle which indicates the noun is the object.	<particle: object "o">	watashi-o	me
particle: past	particle which indicates the past tense.	<particle: past "ta">	ki-ta	came

010

Use the basic structure to talk with Miku! Japanese differentiates formal and casual ways of talking. You use a different style when talking to your friends from asking for something in a shop.
We first provide a casual scene so you can practice to use in the informal situations.
We also have different for girls and boys. You'll find boy a face for words used by boys and a girl face for the girls words. Two faces shows words used by boys and girls.
Role play: Original Miku's voice was recorded.
Enjoy the conversation by taking a role of "kimi" repeating after the voice actors.

Using the same conversation but in the formal situation. Repeat after voiceover recorded by Mai and Shin!

To study further with the basic structure, practice more to speak better!

▶How to Use SONOCA

SONOCA is a music media card developed and maintained by Crypton Future Media, INC. that allows you to download music to your smartphone. It is a new type of media, that combines the appeal of a collectible object and the convenience of a download service.

「SONOCA」（ソノカ）はクリプトン・フューチャー・メディア株式会社が開発・運営するカード型の音楽メディアです。SONOCAを使えばスマホに音楽をダウンロードできます。モノとしてのコレクション性、ダウンロードという利便性をかけ合わせた新しいメディアです。

URL	
How to download	https://sonoca.net/dl/userguide/download
User guide	https://sonoca.net/dl/userguide
Contact	https://sonoca.net/dl/contact

SONOCA
How to download songs

For Smartphone users

STEP1 : SONOCA user registration

1.1 Access the SONOCA webpage (**https://sonoca.net/download**)
1.2 From [**Sign up**], complete listener registration by following the instructions.

STEP2 : Enter the serial code

2.1 Enter the serial code that is written on the back of the SONOCA card, then select [**Next**]
2.2 Select [**OK**] after the track information is displayed
2.3 Click on the App Store icon displayed on the confirmation screen to install the SONOCA app on your device

STEP3 : Download track(s)

3.1 Start your SONOCA app
3.2 Login with your account information you have registered with in STEP1
3.3 Select [**Download**] from the menu (the top left corner of the screen)
3.4 Select the track(s) you want to download
3.5 Click [**Download**] on the download screen

In SONOCA app for Android, the serial code can be scanned using QR code reader.

From the menu (▶ in the upper left icon) , select [**Download**] > [**Activate QR code reader**] to scan the QR code on the back of SONOCA card

From PC

STEP1 : SONOCA user registration

1.1 Access the SONOCA webpage(**https://sonoca.net/download**)
1.2 From [**Sign up**], complete listener registration by following the instructions.

STEP2 : Enter the serial code

2.1 Enter the serial code that is written on the back of the SONOCA card, then select [**Next**]
2.2 Select [**OK**] after the track information is displayed
2.3 Select [**downloading tracks from PC**]

http://sonoca.net/

Haro Hawayu ▶ ハロ／ハワユ

Haro Hawayu ［ハロ／ハワユ］

Have you ever felt you were pathetic or nothing is going well? This song whispers out that feeling when one morning she feels weak and wants to play hooky (but doesn't dare). Better sing so as not to sound too miserable!

▶ Japanese ［日本語］

作詞 ▶ ナノウ
作曲 ▶ ナノウ
唄 ▶ 初音ミク

ハロ 窓を開けて 小さく呟いた

ハワユ 誰もいない 部屋で一人

モーニン 朝が来たよ 土砂降りの朝が

ティクタク 私のネジを 誰か巻いて

ハロ 昔のアニメにそんなのいたっけな

ハワユ 羨ましいな 皆に愛されて

スリーピン 馬鹿な事言ってないで支度をしなくちゃ

クライン 涙の跡を隠す為

Look at page 28.

もう口癖になった「まぁいっか」

昨日の言葉がふと頭を過る

「もう君には全然期待してないから」

そりゃまぁ私だって

自分に期待などしてないけれど

アレは一体どういうつもりですか

> The composer described this song as "a song for the underdogs." In his blog he points to the line that says "nobody pays for the hours you have just existed." But he also wonders why we hesitate to say what we really want to say or what we should say, admitting how weak we are.

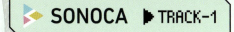

喉元まで出かかった言葉 口をついて出たのは嘘
こうして今日も 私は貴重な 言葉を浪費して生きてゆく

何故隠してしまうのですか 笑われるのが怖いのですか
誰にも会いたくないのですか それ本当ですか
曖昧という名の海に溺れて 息も出来ないほど苦しいの
少し声が聞きたくなりました 本当に弱いな

Haro Hawayu ▶ハロ／ハワユ

Japanese ▶

一向に進まない支度の途中 朦朧とした頭で思う

「もう理由を付けて休んでしまおうかな」

いやいや分かってますって 何となく言ってみただけだよ

分かってるから怒らないでよ

幸せだろうと 不幸せだろうと

平等に 残酷に 朝日は昇る

生きていくだけで 精一杯の私に

これ以上 何を望むというの

Look at page 28.

何故気にしてしまうのですか 本当は愛されたいのですか

その手を離したのは誰ですか 気が付いてますか

人生にタイムカードがあるなら

終わりの時間は何時なんだろう

私が生きた分の給料は 誰が払うんですか

サンキュー ありがとうって言いたいの

サンキュー ありがとうって言いたいよ

サンキュー 一度だけでも良いから

心の底から大泣きしながら

ありがとうって言いたいの

Introduction ▶ 曲紹介

▶ ハロ／ハワユ

何故隠してしまうのですか 本当は聞いて欲しいのですか

絶対に笑ったりしないから 話してみませんか

口を開かなければ分からない 思ってるだけでは伝わらない

なんて面倒くさい生き物でしょう 人間というのは

ハロ ハワユ

あなたに ハロ ハワユ

Roma-ji

Sakushi Nanou
Sakkyoku Nanou
Uta Hatsune Miku

Haro mado-o ake-te chiisaku tsubuya'i-ta
Hawayu daremo ina'i heya-de hitori
Mônin asa-ga ki-ta-yo doshaburi-no asa-ga
Tikutaku watashi-no neji-o dareka ma'i-té

Haro mukashi-no anime-ni sonna-no ita-kke-na
Hawayu urayamashî-na minna-ni aisa-rete
Surîpin baka-na koto itte-naide shitaku-o shina-kucha
Kurain namida-no ato-o kakusu-tame

Mô kuchiguse-ni na-tta "mâ ikka"
Kinô-no kotoba-ga futo atama-o yogiru
"mô kimini-wa zenzen kitaishite ina'i-kara"
Sorya maa watashi-datte
Jibun-ni kita'i nado shite-nai-keredo
Aré-wa itta'i dô yû tsumori-desu-ka

Introduction ▶ 曲紹介

▶ Haro Hawayu

Nodomoto-made dekaka-tta kotoba

Kuchi-o tsui-te deta-nowa uso

Kôshite kyômo watashi-wa kicho-na kotoba-wo rôhishi-te iki-te yuku

Naze kakushi-te-shima'u-no-desu-ka

Warawa-reru-no-ga kowa'i-no-desu-ka

Darenimo aitaku-na'i-no-desu-ka

Sore hontô desu-ka

Aima'i-toi'u na-no umi-ni obore-te

Iki-mo deki-nai-hodo kurushii-no

Sukoshi ko'e-ga kiki-taku-nari-mashi-ta

Hontô-ni yowa'i-na

Haro Hawayu ▶ハロ／ハワユ

Roma-ji ▶

Ikkô-ni susuma-na'i shitaku-no tochû
Môrô-to-shita atama-de omou
"Mô riyû-o tsuke-te yasun-de shi-maou-kana"
Iyaiya waka-tte-masu-tte
Nantonaku itte-mita-dake-dayo
Waka-tteru-kara okora-na'i-deyo

Shiawase-darô-to fushiawase-darô-to
Byôdô-ni zankoku-ni asahi-wa noboru
Ikiteiku-dakede sêippa'i-no watashi-ni
Kore ijô nani-o nozomu-to iuno

Naze kinishite-shimau-no-desu-ka hontô-wa ai-sare-ta'i-no-desu-ka
Sono te-o hanashi-ta-no-wa dare-desuka ki-ga tsui-te-masuka
Jinsê-ni ta'imukâdo-ga aru-nara
Owari-no jikan-wa itsu-nandarô
Watashi-ga ikita bun-no kyûryô-wa dare-ga hara'u-n-desu-ka

Sankyû arigatô-tte î-ta'i-no
Sankyû arigatôtte îta'i-yo
Sankyû ichido-dake-demo î-kara
Kokoro-no soko-kara ônakishi-nagara
Arigatô-tte î-ta'ino

Introduction ▶ 曲紹介

▶ Haro Hawayu

Naze kakushi-te-shima'u-no-desu-ka hontô-wa kii-te-hoshii-no-desu-ka

Zettai-ni wara-ttari shina'i-kara hanashi-te-mimasen-ka

Kuchi-o hiraka-nake-reba wakara-na'i omo-tte-ru-dake-dewa tsutawara-na'i

Nante mendokusai ikimono-deshô ningen-to-iu-no-wa

Haro hawayu

Anata-ni haro hawayu

Translation ▶

▶ Translation [英訳]

Words ▶ Nanou
Music ▶ Nanou
Vocal ▶ Hatsune Miku

"Hello", I opened a window and muttered

"How are you?" to nobody, I'm by myself in the room

"Morning", the morning has come, a morning pouring with rain

Tick-tock, please somebody wind me up

Haro... there's something like that in an old anime

How're you?

Jealously, he was loved by everyone

Sleeping... I shouldn't say a stupid thing; I need to get ready

Crying... to cover up my tear's trace

Got into the habit to say "Well, whatever"

Yesterday's words came back to me,

"I expect nothing from you anymore"

Well, yeah, me too. No hope for myself, but

What did you mean by that?

Introduction ▶曲紹介

▶ Haro Hawayu

A lie came up from my throat and the truth escaped through my lips
Wasting precious words like this, I live like that

Why do you hide it?
Scared of being laughed at?
Don't you want to see anybody?
Is that true?
Drawn in the sea of ambiguity,
it's hard to breathe
I want to hear your voice a little. Damn I'm weak.

Haro Hawayu ▶ ハロ／ハワユ

Translation ▶

I'm stuck in a rut, empty-headed, going nowhere.

"Shall I find an excuse to take the day off?"

Oops, no, I know. I didn't mean it, you know.

I know it! Don't get angry.

Whether happy or sad, the sun also equally on the just and the cruel

I have just enough to live. What more do you expect?

Why do you care?

Don't you want to be loved after all?

Who was it who let go - don't you realize?

If life were a time card, what time would we punch out?

Who would pay the wages for hours I lived?

Thank you, I want to say thank you

Thank you, I want to say thank you

Thank you , even just once,

crying loud from the bottom of the heart, I want to say thank you

Introduction ▶ 曲紹介

▶ Haro Hawayu

Why do you hide it?

Don't you want to be heard after all?

I promise you I won't laugh, so won't you talk to me?

Unless you open your mouth nobody will know. Nobody knows what's on

your mind if you don't tell them.

It's hard work, being human!

Hello, How're you?Hey,

hello, how are you?

Haro Hawayu ▶ハロ／ハワユ

▶ Context and Japanese Culture

文脈と日本の文化
Bunmyaku to Nihon no Bunka

What do you think about this girl? Is she just pretending? Do you understand how she feels? Her attitude in this song is derived from Japanese working conditions which is explained here.

Working Time in Japan(日本の仕事と時間)

▶ In this song...

N	もう	理由を	付けて	休んでしまおうかな
R	mô	riyû-o	tsuke-te	yasun-de shi-maou-kana
E	(now)	find an excuse to	take the day off, shall I?	
M	Shall I find an excuse to take the day off?			

N	人生に	タイムカードが	あるなら
R	jinsê-ni	ta' imukâdo-ga	aru-nara
E	life (in)	time-card	if (be)
M	If life were a time card,		

Whatever,who cares （まあ、いいか）

▶ In this song...

N	まあ、	いっか
R	mâ	ikka
E	well,	whatever
M	well, whatever	

Context and Japanese Culture ▶ 文脈と日本の文化

▶ Analysis

Perspectives on taking time off from work and punctuality in Japan

Although Japanese law guarantees time off from work, half of Japanese people are said they do not take their entitlement of paid holiday, and 60% of people feel guilty about taking their paid holiday. The reasons they gave were that there's not enough staff to cover the extra work, and/or their colleagues are not taking timeoff.

This song is a girl muttering under her breath because she cannot dare to speak up, even for claiming a day off. She even feels her life is calculated like a timecard of the tasks she's been spending her time on.

Key words　「まあ、いっか」/Whatever, who cares/

Literally, "well, whatever" to accept or approve although not fully satisfied. As mentioned above, surprisingly nearly 70% are said they are happy about their paid holidays. Japanese must be survivors, telling themselves that any situation is "ma, ikka."

Tips　仕事と時間 /Work and Time/

Strict punctuality also gives strong pressure in the working environment. You are supposed to be at work, fully prepared to start, five minutes before. This is so that all the meetings start smoothly, all services and jobs are done on time. The problem is that no excuse is allowed: train delays, traffic, even after the great earthquakes people tried to be at work on time.

Haro Hawayu ▶ ハロ／ハワユ

▶ Let's try! Let's practice! Let's talk in Japanese!

日本語で会話してみよう！
Nihongo de kaiwa shitemiyô!

Let's practice greetings in Japanese here. Not only "hello"and "how are you" but there are various greetings depending on the scene, time and people you are greeting to.

▶ Greetings （あいさつ）
基本の挨拶

	☀ morning (down ~ 11:30 a.m.)	☀ sun-set (11:30 a.m. ~)	🌙 sun-set ~ down
N	おはようございます	こんにちは	こんばんは
R	Ohayô gozai-masu	Kon' nichiwa	Kon-banwa
E	Good morning	Good afternoon	Good evening
	morrning （casual）		
N	おはよう		
R	Ohayô		
E	Mornin'		

	💻 work
N	お疲れ様です
R	Otsukare-sama-desu
E	(showing appreciation of hard work) Hi (thanks for working) Bye (thanks for your hard work)

030

Let's try! Let's practice! Let's talk in Japanese! ▶日本語で会話してみよう！

▶ Casual scene

SONOCA ▶ TRACK-11

Morning
朝

ミク：おはよー！
R Miku: Ohayo!

Miku：Mornin'!

きみ：ミクちゃん、おはよ！
R Kimi: Miku-chan, ohayo!

You：Miku, mornin'!

Lunch time
昼

ミク：あ、なにしてるの？
R Miku: A, nani shi-teru-no?

Miku：Hey, what are you doing?

きみ：あ、べつに。
R Kimi: A, betsuni.

You：Well, nothing.

ミク：じゃあ、ご飯食べにいこ？
R Miku: Jâ, gohan tabe-ni iko?

Miku：Well, wanna go to lunch?

きみ：オッケー。
R Kimi: Okke.

You：OK.

Evening
夜

きみ：お疲れー、一緒に帰ろ？
R Kimi: Otskare. issho-ni ka'ero?

You：Worked well. Let's go home together.

ミク：オッケー。ちょっと待ってて。
R Miku: Okke. chotto matte-te.

Miku：OK. Wait for me a moment.

Haro Hawayu ▶ハロ／ハワユ

When saying good-bye (Girls and boys OK)　別れるとき

ミク：じゃあねー、また明日！
🆁 Miku: Jâne, mata ashita!

Miku：Well, then tomorrow!

きみ：じゃあねー。
🆁 Kimi: Jâne.

You：Well, then (bye).

When saying good-bye (Only Boys OK)　別れるとき

きみ：じゃあなー、また明日。
🆁 Kimi: Jâna, mata ashita.

You：Well, then tomorrow.

シン：OK。明日、8時な。
🆁 Shin: Oke. Ashita hachi-ji na.

Shin：OK, tomorrow at eight.

With coworkers at work　同僚と

ミク(senior friend)：おはよー、おつかれー。
🆁 Miku: Ohayô, otsukare.

Miku：Mornin', hello!

きみ (younger)：おつかれさまでーす。
🆁 Kimi: Otsukare-sama dêsu.

You：Hello!

Let's try! Let's practice! Let's talk in Japanese! ▶日本語で会話してみよう！

▶Formal scene

SONOCA ▶ TRACK-12

At a shop
店で

シン：すみません。
R Shin: Sumimasen.

Shin : Excuse me.

店員：はい、いらっしゃいませ。
R Ten'in: Hai. Irasshai-mase.

Clerk : Yes, welcome.

シン：初音ミクのグッズはありますか。
R Shin: Hatsune miku-no guzzu wa ari-masu-ka?

Shin : Do you have goods of Hatsune Miku?

At work
職場で

マイ：おつかれさまです。
R Mai: Otsukare-sama-desu.

Mai : Hello.

鈴木部長：あ、おつかれさま。
　　　　　今日も頑張ってね！
R Suzuki Bucho : A, otsukare-sama. Kyô-mo gamba-tte-né!

Suzuki Manager : Yes. hello. Do your best today, too, won't you?

マイ：はい！頑張ります！
R Mai: Hai, gambari-masu!

Mai : Yes, I'll do my best.

When saying good-bye at the office
帰るとき

シン：お先に失礼します。
R Shin: Osakini shitsurei-shimasu.

Shin : I'm leaving.

マイ：あ、お疲れさまでした。
R Mai: A, otsukare-sama-deshita.

Mai : Well done.

シン：お疲れさまでした。
R Shin: Otukare-sama-deshita.

Shin : Please take care.

033

Desktop Cinderella ▶デスクトップ・シンデレラ

Desktop Cinderella 「デスクトップ・シンデレラ」

This was released in 2015 to celebrate Miku's birthday. All the fans welcomed this song as it sounds so authencically "Hatsune Miku", not only the melody but also the lyrics, where the producers and listeners hear what's in Miku's heart.

▶ Japanese 「日本語」

作詞 八王子P
作曲 八王子P
唄 初音ミク

デスクトップ・シンデレラ

キミと奏でたメロディが

世界を変えていく

どこまでも

Look at page 48.

ひとりぼっちの6畳間

初めてキミの歌を聞いた

小さなモニターに

映るキミは眩しくて

バラバラだった旋律と

言葉を掻き集めたんだ

キミの喜ぶ顔見たくて

Introduction ▶曲紹介

Who do you think "Desktop Cinderella" is? Yes, Hatsune Miku, who sings from the monitor of a desktop PC and who dissapears when it's turned off. This song, however, tells you the melody can change the world. Even though Cinderella's spell was lifted when the clock struck midnight, the VOCALO producer, Hachioji P, emphasised "the magic spell which is not broken at midnight" when he released this song on her birthday in 2015. The song reached a million (viewers) and was recorded in the hall of fame on the day of Miku (3-9, 9th of March) in 2017.

画面の向こうの
大きな世界が
手が届きそうなくらい近くに
感じたんだ

デスクトップ・シンデレラ
あの日の夢の続きを
キミと一緒にいつまでも
見ていたい

デスクトップ・シンデレラ
キミと奏でたメロディが
世界を変えていく
どこまでも

Japanese ▶

頑張り屋さんのキミは
声が枯れるまで歌って
今日も笑顔を届けてる

始まりがあれば
終わりもいつかくる
この時間が永遠に続けば
いいのにな

デスクトップ・シンデレラ
魔法が解けてしまう前に
僕がキミのためにできること
何だろう

デスクトップ・シンデレラ
エレクトリックな愛を
あなたに届けたい
叶うなら

キミにはずいぶん
振り回されたけど
キミがくれた
たくさんのもの
キミがいてくれたから
今の僕がいる

Introduction ▶曲紹介

▶ デスクトップ・シンデレラ

デスクトップ・シンデレラ
12時の鐘が鳴っても
終わらない魔法も
あるんだよ

デスクトップ・シンデレラ
あの日の夢の続きを
キミと一緒にいつまでも
見ていたい

デスクトップ・シンデレラ
キミと奏でたメロディが
世界を変えていく
どこまでも

キミとなら

Desktop Cinderella ▶ デスクトップ・シンデレラ

Roma-ji ▶

Sakushi ▎ Hachioji P
Sakkyoku ▎ Hachioji P
Uta ▎ Hatsune Miku

Desuku-toppu shinderera

Kimi-to kanade-ta merodî-ga

Sekai-o ka'e-te iku

Doko-made-mo

Hitoribocchi-no rokujôma

Hajimete kimi-no uta-o kîta

Chîsana monitâ-ni

Utsuru kimi-wa mabushiku-te

Barabara-datta senritsu-to

Kotoba-o kaki-atsume-tan-da

Kimi-no yorokobu ka'o mi-taku-te

Introduction ▶ 曲紹介

▶ Desktop Cinderella

Gamen-no mukô-no

Ôki-na seka'i-ga

Te-ga todokisôna-kurai chikaku-ni

Kanji-ta-nda

Desukutoppu shinderera

Ano hi-no yume-no tsuzuki-o

Kimi-to issho-ni itsumade-mo

Mite-ita'i

Desukutoppu shinderera

Kimi-to kanade-ta merodî-ga

Seka'i-o ka'ete-iku

Doko-made-mo

Desktop Cinderella ▶ デスクトップ・シンデレラ

Roma-ji ▶

Gambari-ya-san-no kimi-wa

Ko'e-ga kareru-made uta-tte

Kyo-mo ega'o-o todoke-teru

Hajimari-ga aré-ba

Owari-mo itsuka kuru

Kono jikan-ga e'ien-ni tsuzuke-ba

Ii-no-ni-na

Desukutoppu shinderera

Mahô-ga toke-te-shimau ma'e-ni

Boku-ga kimi-no tame-ni dekiru koto

Nan-darô

Desukutoppu shinderera

Erekutorikku-na a'i-o

Anata-ni todoke-ta'i

Kana'u-nara

Kimi-ni-wa zuibun

Furi-mawasa-re-ta kedo

Kimi-ga kure-ta

Takusan-no mono

Kimi-ga ite kure-ta kara

Ima-no boku-ga iru

Introduction ▶ 曲紹介

▶ デスクトップ・シンデレラ

Desukutoppu shinderera

Jûni-ji-no kane-ga na-tte-mo

Owara-na'i mahô-mo

Aru-n-da-yo

Desukutoppu shinderera

Ano hi-no yume-no tsuzuki-o

Kimi-to issho-ni itsu-made-mo

Mi-te-ita'i

Desukutoppu shinderera

Kimi-to kanade-ta merodî-ga

Sekai-o ka'e-te-iku

Doko-made-mo

Kimi-to-nara

Desktop Cinderella ▶デスクトップ・シンデレラ

Translation ▶

▶Translation 〔 英訳 〕

Words Hachioji P
Music Hachioji P
Vocal Hatsune Miku

Desktop Cinderella

The melody I played with you

Continues to change the world

Endlessly

Alone in the six-tatami room

Introduction ▶ 曲紹介

▶ Desktop Cinderella

Beyond the screen,

The huge world

Is close enough within my reach

That's how I felt

Desktop Cinderella

A sequel of the dream of that day

With you, forever

I want to see

Desktop Cinderella

The melody I played with you

Continues to change the world

Endlessly

Desktop Cinderella ▶デスクトップ・シンデレラ

Translation ▶

You as a hard-worker

Always sing until your voice gives out

And deliver your smile today, too

If there's a beginning,

Then an end will come someday

I wish this time would last forever

Desktop Cinderella

Before the spell breaks

What can I do for you,

I wonder?

Desktop Cinderella

Electric love

Is what I want to deliver

If possible

Even though you've been

Spun around so much

You gave me

Lots of things

And you stay with me

That's why I'm who I am now.

Introduction 曲紹介

▶ Desktop Cinderella

Desktop Cinderella
Even when the clock bell struck midnight
There's a spell which never breaks

Desktop Cinderella
A sequel of the dream of that day
With you, forever
I want to see

Desktop Cinderella
The melody I played with you
Keeps changing the world
Endlessly

With you

Illustration by TNSK
© Crypton Future Media, INC. www.piapro.net
© 壁の彩度

Desktop Cinderella ▶デスクトップ・シンデレラ

▶▶ Context and Japanese Culture

文脈と日本の文化
Bunmyaku to Nihon no Bunka

There are some foreign origin words here. The pronunciation of such words are similar but need to follow a rule; a consonant has to be followed by a vowel. Thus "desktop"comes "desukutoppu" and "melody" becomes "merodî". Let's see more details!

外来語／カタカナ (Foreign origin words & katakana)

▶ In this song...

N	デスクトップ
R	desuku-toppu
E	desktop

N	モニター
R	monitâ
E	monitor

N	メロディ
R	merodî
E	melody

048

Context and Japanese Culture ▶ 文脈と日本の文化

▶ Analysis

外来語／カタカナ (Foreign origin words & katakana)

There are many words of foreign origin. "Gairai-go", loan words mainly from the Western countries are usually written in "katakana". The meaning of loan words are associated with products, things, person or phenomenon which was imported but might have been modified or misunderstood.

Key words Kimi/キミ

"kimi", meaning "you" is often written in katakana. Why? Katakana is actually used not only for foreign words but also when describing something which makes us feel distance, respects, or emphasis. When "kimi" is written in katakana we would feel cool and a bit of distance. Plus, we have many more ways to describe "you", the second person pronoun, in Japanese.

N	R	M
あなた	anata	the most general way. It sounds rude to indicate a person to his face.
きみ／君／キミ	kimi	casual way, used by a boy or pretentiously boy-like girl.
おまえ	oma'e	very frank way, usually used by a male.
おたく	otaku	originally the word was created by combining "o" (an honorific prefix) and "taku" (home), now used by the older generation as the 2nd person pronoun while younger generation use it to describe people who tend to stay at home with particular interests in manga, anime, games without much socializing with real people.

Tips IT words in Japanese

When computers and the concepts were imported many of the words came to Japan without being translated to Japanese. "Computer" is "kompûtâ", "monitor" is "monitâ".

Later those words were shortened for ease of pronunciation. For example, "personal computer" was abbreviated to "paso-kon" from "pâsonaru kompûtâ".Other digital related loan words are: デジタル（**R**dejital,**E**digital）, ノートPC（**R**nôtoPC,**E**laptop PC）, ネット（**R**netto,**E**internet）.

Desktop Cinderella ▶デスクトップ・シンデレラ

▶ Let's try! Let's practice! Let's write in Japanese!

日本語で書いてみよう！

Nihongo de kaite miyô!

You can learn many basic Japanese words from this song. Katakana is the easiest way to write Japanese. Let's practice some words（→ Look at the page 196, "カタカナ50音表"）.

▶ Katakana-hyô （カタカナ表）

ワ wa	ラ ra	ヤ ya	マ ma	ハ ha	ナ na	タ ta	サ sa	カ ka	ア a
	リ ri		ミ mi	ヒ hi	ニ ni	チ chi	シ shi	キ ki	イ i
ヲ o	ル ru	ユ yu	ム mu	フ fu	ヌ nu	ツ tsu	ス su	ク ku	ウ u
	レ re		メ me	ヘ he	ネ ne	テ te	セ se	ケ ke	エ e
ン n	ロ ro	ヨ yo	モ mo	ホ ho	ノ no	ト to	ソ so	コ ko	オ o

050

Let's try! Let's practice! Let's write in Japanese! ▶日本語で書いてみよう！

▶ Let's write katakana! ~Words in the song~

ミク　　R miku　　E miku

デスクトップ　R desukutoppu　E desktop

シンデレラ　R shinderera　E cinderella

モニター　R monitâ　E monitor

Desktop Cinderella ▶デスクトップ・シンデレラ

▶Let's write katakana! ~ Countries in the world ~

アメリカ   **R** amerika   **E** America

イギリス   **R** igirisu   **E** England

インドネシア   **R** indoneshia   **E** Indonesia

チャイナ   **R** Chaina   **E** China

タイ   **R** Tai   **E** Thai

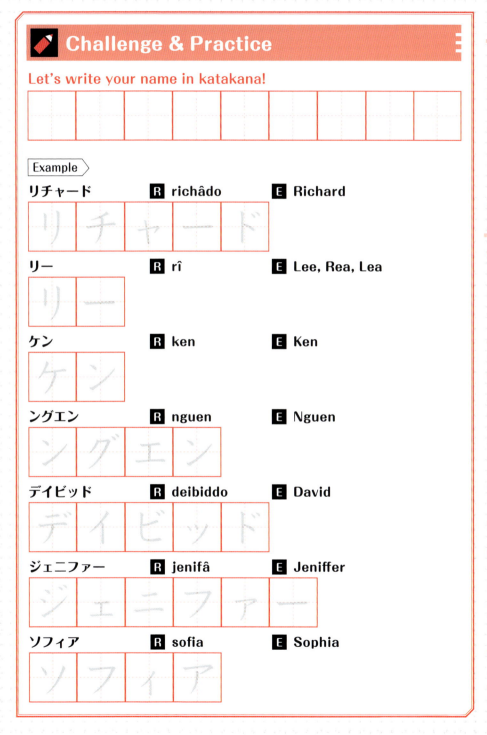

Haru ga kita 　春が来た

VOCALO P, "Kuroda Ashin" produced this song for this book based on the popular nursery song, "Spring has come". The song describes the joy of spring. Sing along and see how the natural world changes with the arrival of spring in Japan!

▶ Japanese [日本語]

作詞 ▶ 高野辰之
作曲 ▶ 岡野貞一
編曲 ▶ 黒田亜津
唄 ▶ 初音ミク

春が来た 春が来た どこに来た

山に来た 里に来た

野にも来た

Look at page 62.

花が咲く 花が咲く どこに咲く

山に咲く 里に咲く

野にも咲く

Introduction ▶ 曲紹介

The song was composed for elementary school students and published in the official school song book in 1910. It is sung in February when the weather is still cold, and people are looking forward to the warmer spring days.

 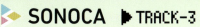
SONOCA ▶ TRACK-3

鳥が鳴く 鳥が鳴く どこで鳴く
山で鳴く 里で鳴く
野でも鳴く

`Look at page 62.`

春が来た 春が来た どこに来た
山に来た 里に来た
野にも来た

花が咲く 花が咲く どこに咲く
山に咲く 里に咲く
野にも咲く

鳥が鳴く 鳥が鳴く どこで鳴く
山で鳴く 里で鳴く
野でも鳴く

057

Roma-ji ▶

▶Roma-ji ［ローマ字］

Sakushi ▶ Takano Tatsuyuki
Sakkyoku ▶ Okano Teiichi
Henkyoku ▶ Kuroda Ashin
Uta ▶ Hatsune Miku

Haru-ga ki-ta haru-ga ki-ta doko-ni ki-ta

Yama-ni ki-ta sato-ni ki-ta

No-ni-mo ki-ta

Hana-ga saku hana-ga saku doko-ni saku

Yama-ni saku sato-ni saku

No-ni-mo saku

Introduction ▶ 曲紹介

▶ Haru ga kita

Tori-ga naku tori-ga naku doko-de naku
Yama-de naku sato-de naku
No-de-mo naku

Illustration by おがこ ろろみ
© Crypton Future Media, INC. www.piapro.ne

Haru ga kita ▶春が来た

Translation ▶

▶Translation [英訳]

Words ▸ Takano Tatsuyuki
Music ▸ Okano Teiichi
Arranged ▸ Ashin Kuroda
Vocal ▸ Hatsune Miku

Spring has come, spring has come. Where is spring?

Spring has come to the mountains;

Spring has come to the villages

Spring has come to the fields as well

Flowers are blossoming, flowers are blossoming,

where are they blossoming?

Flowers are blossoming in the mountains,

flowers are blossoming in the villages

Flowers are blossoming in the fields as well.

Introduction ▶ 曲紹介

▶ Haru ga kita

Birds are singing, birds are singing, where are they singing?
Birds are singing in the mountains, birds are singing in the villages
Birds are singing in the fields as well

Illustration by CoPe
© Crypton Future Media, INC. www.piapro.net piapro

Haru ga kita ▶ 春が来た

▶ Context and Japanese Culture

文脈と日本の文化
Bunmyaku to Nihon no Bunka

After winter, we welcome spring with joy as much as people in other countries. This simple nursery rhyme contains those feelings for the nature in Japan.

Spring in Japan （日本の春）

▶ In this song...

N	春が	来た
R	Haru-ga	kita
E	Spring	has come
M	Spring has come	

N	花が	咲く
R	Hana-ga	saku
E	Flower(s)	blossom
M	Flower(s) blossom.	

N	鳥が	鳴く
R	Tori-ga	naku
E	Bird(s)	sing
M	Birds are singing.	

Context and Japanese Culture ▶ 文脈と日本の文化

▶ Analysis

Symbols of Spring in Japan

At the time this song was composed, the symbols of early spring in February were plum blossoms and bush-warblers. These days we have an image of cherry blossoms in the warm days of March or tulips for children when we think of spring. The bush-warbler or "uguisu" are one of the 春告鳥 "harutsuge-dori", a bird which announces the (arrival of) spring.

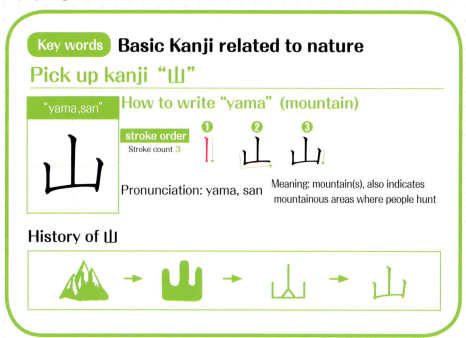

Tips Spring Flowers in Japan

Plum is the first to blossom in the end of winter in February, followed by the beautiful peach blossoms in early March, often used to decorate Girls Day or the Doll Festival on 3rd of March. It is hard to know exactly when Sakura or cherry blossom, will be in bloom, but it is usually after peach blossoms. Plum, peach and cherry blossoms have always been symbols of spring in Japan. Nowadays, tulips and rape blossoms are also associated with spring.

Haru ga kita ▶春が来た

▶ Let's try! Let's practice! Let's talk in Japanese!

日本語で会話してみよう！

Nihongo de kaiwa shitemiyô!

Let's learn how to form the past tense in Japanese. This song describes a joy of the arrival of spring and Japanese past tense particle "ta".

▶基本構文

❶「動詞」＋た／「形容詞」＋た（past）

R [verb] + ta/[adj] + ta

E [te-form] + [particle：ta (past)]

The particle "ta" can follow a verb or an adjective to describe the past and perfect tense.
The verb which is followed by "ta" conjugates as "te-form". (→ P.192)
"ta" changes to a voiced sound "da" with certain verbs and adjectives.

064

Let's try! Let's practice! Let's talk in Japanese! ▶日本語で会話してみよう！

▶ Casual scene   ▶ SONOCA ▶ TRACK-13

きみ：レンはもう来た？
R Kimi: Ren-wa mô ki-ta?

You : Has Ren come yet?

ミク：まだ。
R Miku: Mada.

Miku : Not yet.

きみ：遅いねぇ。ミクは、昨日、何した？
R Kimi: Osoi-nê. Miku-wa, kinô nani shi-ta?

You : So late...Miku, what did you do yesterday?

ミク：昨日は、本を読んだよ。
R Miku: Kinô wa hon-o yon-dayo.

Miku : I read a book yesterday.

きみ：おもしろかった？
R Kimi: Omoshiro-ka-tta?

You : Interesting?

ミク：うん、すごくおもしろかった。
R Miku: Un, sugoku omoshiro-ka-tta.

Miku : Yeah, it was super interesting.

065

Haru ga kita ▶春が来た

▶ Formal scene

SONOCA ▶ TRACK-14

マイ：レンさんはもう来ましたか？

R Mai: Ren-san wa mô kimashi-ta-ka?

Mai： Has Ren-san come yet?

シン：いいえ、まだです。

R Shin: îe, mada-desu.

Shin： Not, yet.

マイ：遅いですね。シンさん、昨日は、何をしましたか？

R Mai: Osoi-desu-né. Shin-san, kinô-wa nani-o shi-mashi-ta-ka?

Mai： He's late...Shin-san, what did you do yesterday?

シン：昨日は、本を読みました。

R Shin:Kinô wa hon-o yomi-mashi-ta.

Shin： I read a book yesterday.

マイ：おもしろかったですか？

R Mai: Omoshiro-ka-tta-desu-ka?

Mai： Was it interesting?

シン：はい、とてもおもしろかったです。

R Shin:Hai,totemo omoshiro-ka-tta-desu.

Shin： Yes, it was so interesting.

066

Let's try! Let's practice! Let's talk in Japanese! ▶日本語で会話してみよう！

 Challenge & Practice

Choose a verb(past tense) from the Option and fill [A] to complete the conversation like the example.

N あなた：レンはもう［ A ］？
　　ミク：まだ。

R Anata：Ren wa mô ［ A ］ ?
　　Miku：Mada.

E You：Has Ren ［ A ］ yet ?
　　Miku：Not yet.

Example　　あなた：レンはもう［ 来た ］？
　　　　　　　ミク：まだ。

Options

	dictionary form		te-form + "ta"
❶	たべる	**R** taberu **E** eat	❶
❷	おわる	**R** owaru **E** finish	❷
❸	うたう	**R** utau **E** sing	❸

Model Answer
❶　たべた　　**R** tabeta　　**E** ate
❷　おわった　**R** owatta　　**E** finished
❸　うたった　**R** utatta　　**E** sang

067

Hajimete no oto ▶ハジメテノオト

Hajimete no oto 「ハジメテノオト」

The song is sung in a slow tempo to express the feelings of the VOCALOID. When you sing, feel the contrast between the "VOCALOID", who is eternal, and the "human" who changes as time goes by. This song has been popular for more than ten years for its warm lyrics and melody.

▶ Japanese 「日本語」

作詞 ▌ malo
作曲 ▌ malo
唄 ▌ 初音ミク

初めての音は　なんでしたか？

あなたの　初めての音は…

ワタシにとっては　これがそう

だから　今　うれしくて

初めての言葉は　なんでしたか？

あなたの　初めての言葉

ワタシは言葉って　言えない

だから　こうしてうたっています

やがて日が過ぎ　年が過ぎ

世界が　色あせても

あなたがくれる　灯りさえあれば

いつでも　ワタシはうたうから

Introduction ▶曲紹介

This song has been popular since its first release in 2007. Mysteriously, the original post still has no name of who produced it, but expediently "malo" who appears as in "malo feat. Hatsune Miku" outside of Niko Niko, has been credited.

This is a ballad, which expresses the sorrow of being a VOCALOID. The lyric "I cannot deliver with words but I can sing a song" describes exactly the VOCALOID state of existence.

It is one of the Million-views videos among original VOCALOID songs.

空の色も　風のにおいも
海の深さも　あなたの声も
ワタシは知らない　だけど歌を
歌をうたう　ただ声をあげて

なにかあなたに　届くのなら
何度でも　何度だって
かわらないわ　あのときのまま
ハジメテノオトのまま…

Look at page 82.

Hajimete no oto ▶ ハジメテノオト

Japanese ▶

初めての音は　ありましたか？

あなたの　初めての音は…

知らない曲とか　街の音に

ワクワクしてますか？

初めての言葉は　ありましたか？

あなたの　初めての言葉

言えずにしまったり　言わなかった

言葉は　少しさみしそう

やがて日が過ぎ　年が過ぎ

古い荷物も　ふえて

あなたが　かわっても

失くしたくないものは

ワタシに　あずけてね

時の流れも　傷の痛みも

愛の深さも　あなたの声も

ワタシは知らない　だけど歌は

歌はうたえるわ　だからきいて

Introduction ▶曲紹介

▶ハジメテノオト

もしもあなたが　望むのなら

何度でも　何度だって

かわらないわ　あのときのまま

ハジメテノオトのまま…

空の色も　風のにおいも

海の深さも　ワタシのうたも

かわらないわ　あのときのまま

ハジメテノオトのまま…

初めての音に　なれましたか？

あなたの　初めての音に

世界のどこでも　ワタシはうたう

それぞれの　ハジメテノオトを…

Roma-ji

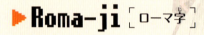

▶ Roma-ji [ローマ字]

Sakushi malo
Sakkyoku malo
Uta Hatsune Miku

Hajimete-no oto-wa nan-deshi-ta-ka?

Anata-no hajimete-no oto-wa...

Watashi-ni-totte-wa kore-ga sô

Dakara ima ureshiku-te

Hajimete-no kotoba-wa nan-deshi-ta-ka?

Anata-no hajimete-no kotoba

Watashi-wa kotoba-tte ie-nai

Dakara kôshite uta-tte-imasu

Yagate hi-ga sugi toshi-ga sugi

Sekai-ga iroase-te-mo

Anata-ga kureru akari-sae are-ba

Itsudemo watashi-wa utau-kara

Introduction ▶ 曲紹介

▶ Hajimete no oto

Sora-no iro-mo, kaze-no ni'oi-mo

Umi-no fukasa-mo anata-no koe-mo

Watashi-wa shira-nai dakedo uta-o

Uta-o utau tada koe-o agé-te

Nani-ka anata-ni todoku-no-nara

Nando-demo nando-datte

Kawara-naiwa anotoki-no mama

Hajimete-no oto-no mama...

Roma-ji ▶

Hajimete-no oto-wa ari-mashi-ta-ka?

Anata-no hajimete-no oto-wa...

Shira-nai kyoku-toka machi-no oto-ni

Wakuwaku shite-masu-ka?

Hajimete-no kotoba-wa ari-mashita-ka?

Anata-no hajimete-no kotoba

Ie-zu-ni shima-ttari iwa-naka-tta

Kotoba-wa sukoshi samisi-sô

Yagate hi-ga sugi, toshi-ga sugi

Furui nimotsu-mo fue-te

Anata-ga kawa-ttemo

Nakushi-taku-nai mono-wa

Watashi-ni azuke-te-né

Toki-no nagare-mo, kizu-no itami-mo

A'i-no fukasa-mo, anata-no ko'e-mo

Watashi-wa shira-nai dakedo uta-wa

Uta-wa utae-ru-wa dakara ki-ité

Introduction ▶ 曲紹介

▶ Hajimete no oto

Moshimo anata-ga nozomu-no-nara

Nando-demo nando-datte

Kawara-nai-wa ano toki-no mama

Hajimete-no oto-no mama...

Sora-no iro-mo kaze-no ni'oi-mo

Umi-no fukasa-mo watashi-no uta-mo

Kawara-nai-wa ano toki-no mama

Hajimete-no oto-no mama...

Hajimete-no oto-ni nare-mashita-ka?

Anata-no hajimete-no oto-ni

Sekai-no doko-demo watashi-wa uta'u

Sorezore-no hajimete-no oto-o...

Hajimete no oto ▶ ハジメテノオト

Translation ▶

▶ Translation [英訳]

Words	malo
Music	malo
Vocal	Hatsune Miku

What was your first sound?

Your first sound (you heard)?

For me, this is the one

That is why, now I'm so happy...

What was your first word?

Your first word?

I do not speak with words

That is why I sing this way

Days pass, years pass

The world loses its colours

But as long as you give me light

Anytime, I sing...

Introduction ▶曲紹介

▶ Hajimete no oto

The colour of the sky, and the smell of the wind...

The depth of the sea and the sound of your voice,

Things I do not know, but the song...

I sing a song, lifting my voice

As long as it reaches you

However many times, so many times

It doesn't change; it's just like that time...

That time of "my First Sound"

Hajimete no oto ▶ ハジメテノオト

Translation ▶

Do you have a "First Sound"?

Ever had your own First Sound?

An unknown tune, or the sound of a city...

Is it now exciting you?

Do you have a "First Sound"?

Ever had your own First Sound?

Words you locked away in your mind without speaking, never spoken,

Those words, they look a little sad

Days pass, years pass

More baggage from your past

Even if you change

Those things you do not want to lose,

Give them to me

The flow of the time, the hurt and the wounds

The depth of love, the sound of your voice

These things I do not know... but songs...

I can sing songs, so listen to me

Introduction ▶曲紹介

▶ Hajimete no oto

If you really wish

However many times, however often,

It doesn't change, it's just like that time,

Like that time of the "First Sound"

The colour of the sky, and the smell of the wind...

The depth of the sea, the songs I sing,

It doesn't change, it's just like that time,

Like that time of the "First Sound"

Could I become your First Sound?

Your First Sound?

Wherever in the world, I sing

Everywhere has its own first sound

ハジメテノオト

Hajimete no oto ▶ハジメテノオト

▶ Context and Japanese Culture

文脈と日本の文化
Bunmyaku to Nihon no Bunka

As Miku sings what she cannot feel, the song describes Japanese sensitivity to the nature.

Sensitivity (繊細さ)

▶In this song...

N	空の色も	風のにおいも	海の深さも
R	sora-no iro-mo	kaze-no ni'oi-mo	umi-no fukasa-mo
E	colour of sky-[particle : mo]	smell of wind-[particle : mo]	depth of sea-[particle : mo]

N	あなたの声も	ワタシは知らない
R	anata-no koe-mo	watashi-wa shiranai
E	voice of yours	I don't know
M	I don't know either the colour of the sky, the smell of the wind, and the depth of the ocean or (the sound of) your voice.	

082

Context and Japanese Culture ▶ 文脈と日本の文化

▶ Analysis

Japanese sensitivity to nature, colour, smell, feeling...

The sky has many different colours depending on the area, humidity, and other factors. Deep in the Japanese culture there lies the strong belief that all natural phenomena are deities. The sky was the home of powerful gods of Thunder, Wind and the Sun Goddess herself.

In the song, Miku says she does not know the colour of the sky, nor the smell of the wind. She is a virtual singer. Even as the world changes, she is unchangeable. She is beyond time and place.

Key words 初めての / first

"Hajimete-no oto" and "Hatsune" mean the same!

The Japanese character 初 has several pronunciations in Japanese; /hatsu/, /haji/, /sho/.The core meaning of the character is 'the first' or 'new'.

The character 音 : Pronunciation in Japanese: /oto/, /ne/, /on/, meaning sound, note (music), noise. Thus 初めての音 /Hajimete-no oto/ means the first sound, while Miku's family name 初音 /hatsu ne/ can also mean the first sound.

Tips Four sets of JAPANESE writing and their roles

Japanese consists of four writing systems: hiragana, katakana, kanji, ro-maji. Each has different roles. Japanese texts are normally written with a combination of hiragana, katakana and kanji. Hiragana and katakana (and Romaji) symbolise the sound, like the alphabet, while kanji is an ideogram. Katakana is used to transcribe loan words, foreign proper nouns and onomatopoeia, for sounds without meaning. To the Japanese, this gives katakana a 'foreign' or 'alien' feel, as in conversations with foreign people, robots and unknown creatures like spaceman. As "Hajimete-no oto" is written in katakana, it gives the image of futuristic robot. And because it does not use the kanji you cannot get the immediate and direct connection to Hatsune.

Hajimete no oto ▶ハジメテノオト

▶Let's try! Let's practice! Let's talk in Japanese!

日本語で会話してみよう！

Nihongo de kaiwa shitemiyô!

You can learn many basic Japanese words from this song. It'll also tell you how Miku feels as a VOCALOID, and how she feels the difference between VOCALOID and humans.

▶基本構文

❶ 初めて

R Hajimete
E first time

❷ 初めての「 名詞 」

R Hajimete no + [noun]
E first + [noun]

❸ 初めて「 動詞 」

R Hajimete (adv.) + [verb]
E first time + [verb]

Let's try! Let's practice! Let's talk in Japanese! ▶日本語で会話してみよう！

▶ Casual scene   ▶ SONOCA ▶ TRACK-15

ミク：日本は初めて？
R Miku：Nihon-wa hajimete?

Miku：First trip to Japan?

きみ：うん、初めて。これが、私の初めての海外旅行。
R Kimi：Un, hajimete. Kore-ga watasi-no hajimete-no kaigairyokô.

You：Yeah, first time. This is my first trip abroad.

ミク：じゃあ、私のコンサートも初めて？
R Miku：Ja, watashi-no konsâto-mo hajimete?

Miku：Then, first time to my concert?

きみ：ううん、アメリカで行ったよ。これは2回目だよ。
R Kimi：Uun, amerika-de, itta-yo. Kore-wa ni-kaime-dayo.

You：Noop. I went to one in the US. This is my second time.

085

Hajimete no oto ▶ハジメテノオト

▶Formal scene

SONOCA ▶ TRACK-16

シン：日本は初めてですか？

R Shin: Nihon-wa hajimete-desu-ka?

マイ：はい、初めてです。これが、私の初めての海外旅行です。

R Mai: Hai, hajimete-desu. Kore-ga watashi-no hajimete-no kaigai ryokô desu.

シン：じゃあ、私のコンサートも初めてですか？

R Shin: Ja, watashi-no konsâto-mo hajimete desu-ka?

マイ：いいえ、アメリカで行きました。これは２回目です。

R Mai: Iie, amerika-de iki-mashi-ta. Kore-wa ni kaime-desu.

Shin : Is this your first trip to Japan?

Mai : Yes, first time. This is my first trip abroad.

Shin : Then, is this your first time to my concert?

Mai : No. I went to one in the US. This is my second time.

086

Let's try! Let's practice! Let's talk in Japanese! ▶日本語で会話してみよう！

Challenge & Practice

Use the expressions of frequency to complete the conversations.

Example1 初めて (first time)

これは 私の 初めての 日本旅行です。

R Kore-wa watashi-no hajimete-no nihon ryokô-desu.

E This is my first trip to Japan.

Practice1 Practice by filling the brackets. Choose from the options [A] below.

これは、私の初めての「　　A　　」です。

R Kore-wa watashi-no hajimete-no [　　A　　] desu.

E This is my first [　　A　　].

Example2 2回目、3回目…(second, third… time)

これは 私の 2回目の 日本旅行です。

R Kore-wa watashi-no ni-kaime-no nihon ryokô-desu.

E This is second-time trip to Japan.

Practice2 Practice by filling the brackets. Choose from the options [A] and [B] below.

これは、私の「　　B　　」回目の「　　A　　」です。

R Kore-wa watashi-no [　　B　　] kaime-no [　　A　　] desu.

E This is my 2nd (3rd, 4th, 5th…)[　　A　　].

Options A

N	R	E
海外旅行	kaigai ryokô	trip to another country
ミクのコンサート	miku-no konsâto	Miku's concert
お茶会	ochakai	Tea Ceremony
日本語レッスン	nihongo ressun	Japanese language lesson

Options B

2回目	ni-ka'ime	2nd	4回目	yon-ka'ime	4th
3回目	san-ka'ime	3rd	5回目	go-ka'ime	5th

Saihate ▶ サイハテ

Saihate

[サイハテ]

The Japanese words here are easy to learn and understand, but there's a
a little sadness behind the happy melody.
Can you notice this when you sing?

▶Japanese [日本語]

作詞▶小林オニキス
作曲▶小林オニキス
唄▶初音ミク

むこうはどんな所なんだろうね？
無事に着いたら　便りでも欲しいよ

扉を開いて　彼方へと向かうあなたへ
この歌声と祈りが　届けばいいなぁ

雲ひとつないような　抜けるほど晴天の今日は
悲しいくらいに　お別れ日和で

ありふれた人生を　紅く色付ける様な
たおやかな恋でした　たおやかな恋でした

さよなら

Introduction ▶ 曲紹介

The song is about the moment that we cannot avoid, when we must say goodbye to somebody forever. Onyx, the VOCALOID Producer, combined the light melody and the lyrics of forever departing to establish the new genre as pop-requiem. Significantly, it was released on the day before the 13th memorial day of the Great Hanshin-Awaji Earthquake. The song is one of the million-sellers of the original VOCALOID songs.

またいつの日にか　出会えると信じられたら
これからの日々も　変わらず　やり過ごせるね

扉が閉まれば　このまま離ればなれだ
あなたの煙は　雲となり雨になるよ

Look at page 96.

ありふれた人生を　紅く色付ける様な
たおやかな恋でした　たおやかな恋でした

さよなら

Roma-ji ▶

▶ Roma-ji [ローマ字]

Sakushi ▶ Kobayashi onyx
Sakkyoku ▶ Kobayashi onyx
Uta ▶ Hatsune Miku

Mukô-wa don'na tokoro nan-darô-né
Bujini tsui-tara tayori-demo hoshî-yo

Tobira-o hirai-te kanata-e-to mukáu anata-e
Kono utagoe-to inori-ga todoke-ba î-na

Kumo hitotsu nai-yô-una nukeru-hodo seiten-no kyo-wa
Kanashî-kurai-ni owakare-biyori-de

Arifure-ta jinsei-o akaku irozukeru yô-na
Taoyakana koi deshi-ta taoyakana koi deshi-ta

Sayonara

Introduction ▶曲紹介

▶ Saihate

Mata itsuno hi-ni-ka dea-eru-to shinji-rare-tara
Kore-kara-no hibi-mo kawara-zu yarisugose-ru-ne

Tobira-ga shimare-ba konomama hanarebanare-da
Anata-no kemuri-wa kumo-to nari ame-ni naru-yo

Arifure-ta jinsei-o akaku irozukeru yô-na
Taoyakana koi deshi-ta taoyakana koi deshi-ta

Sayonara

Saihate ▶ サイハテ

Translation ▶

 [英訳]

Words ▶ Kobayashi onyx
Music ▶ Kobayashi onyx
Vocal ▶ Hatsune Miku

I wonder what kind of place over there could be?
I want to hear that you got there safe

To you who open the doors to go over there
I wish my song and prayers would reach

So sad a goodbye on such a sunny day

Such an ordinary life was mine, bathed in a red glow,
such a graceful love

Sayonara

Introduction 曲紹介

▶ **Saihate**

If I can believe I can see you again some day,
I can endure the days ahead

When the doors close, we will be parted just like that,
The smoke of your body will become clouds and then rain

Such an ordinary life was mine, bathed in a red glow,
such a graceful love

Sayonara

Illustration by 小林オニキス
© Crypton Future Media, INC. www.piapro.net piapro

Saihate ▶ サイハテ

▶ Context and Japanese Culture

文脈と日本の文化
Bunmyaku to Nihon no Bunka

Let's learn about Japanese culture and attitudes to life with this song. Miku's songs are even better when you can understand their true meaning.

Death (死) ／ Bereavement (死別)

▶ In this song...

N	扉が	閉まれば	このまま	離ればなれだ
R	tobira-ga	shimare-ba	konomama	hanarebanare-da
E	the door	if closed	like that	will be parted
M	when the doors close, we will be parted just like that			

N	あなたの	煙は	雲	と　なり	雨に	なるよ
R	anata-no	kemuri-wa	kumo	to nari	ame-ni	naru-yo
E	your	smoke	clouds	will become and	then rain	will become
M	The smoke of your body will become clouds and then rain					

Reincarnation (生まれ変わり)

▶ In this song...

N	また	いつの	日にか	出会えると	信じられたら
R	mata	itsu-no	hi-ni-ka	de'a-e-ru-to	shinji-rare-tara
E	again	someday		I can see (you)	if I can
M	If I can believe I can see you again someday,				

096

Context and Japanese Culture ▶ 文脈と日本の文化

▶ Analysis

Perspectives on death and life

In Japan, the dead are usually cremated, so "the smoke of your body","the doors close", or "I wish I can see you again" are very strong images. The lyric depicts bereavement and we can imagine the doors closing after the coffin. (There are differences depending on the local customs). The song also thinks about reincarnation, which is one of beliefs in Japanese culture, although opinions vary and many Japanese doubt the existence of a "next world" .

Key words たおやかな /Taoyakana/

嫋やか (na-adjective). The kanji combines the characters for woman and weak, but it does not mean weakness. The adjective came to describe a woman's graceful movement and the woman herself. The word was widely used in medieval literature but is not common these days.

Tips さいはて /sai hate/

Literally it could mean the geographical edge of the land, but it also implies the end of life. "hate-ru", the verb form of "hate" could mean "to die". Sometimes translated (in YouTube, for example) as "far away" which could also imply emotional remoteness, but when the two characters are used together in Japanese as "sai-hate" it always conveys a certain sadness.

Saihate ▶サイハテ

▶ Let's try! Let's practice! Let's talk in Japanese!

日本語で会話してみよう！
Nihongo de kaiwa shitemiyô!

Let's learn how to ask places, how to describe what you want using phrases from the song. They are useful for conversation with friends as well as at a shop in Japan!

▶ 基本構文

❶ 〜はどんなところ？

R [Name of the place] + [particle : wa]+don-na tokoro?

E What kind of place is [name of the place] …?

❷ 〜がほしい。

R [noun] + [particle : ga] + hoshii.

E I want [noun] .

098

Let's try! Let's practice! Let's talk in Japanese! ▶日本語で会話してみよう！

▶ Casual scene

きみ：秋葉原ってどんなところかな？
R Kimi : Akihabara-tte don-na tokoro-kana?

You : What kind of place is Akihabara, I wonder?

ミク：アニメで有名なところだよ。
R Miku : Anime-de yūmei-na tokoro dayo.

Miku : The place where anime is famous.

きみ：ええ、ほんとう？
R Kimi : Ee honto?

You : Oh, really?

ミク：アニメグッズもたくさんあるよ。
R Miku : Anime guzzu mo takusan aru-yo.

Miku : There is a lot of anime goods.

きみ：アニメグッズ、ほしいなあ。
R Kimi : Anime guzzu, hoshii naa.

You : I want anime goods.

Illustration by 小林オニキス
© Crypton Future Media, INC. www.piapro.net

099

Formal scene

SONOCA ▶ TRACK-18

シン：秋葉原ってどんなところですか？
Shin：Akihabara-tte don-na tokoro desu-ka?

マイ：アニメで有名なところですよ。
Mai：Anime-de yûmei-na tokoro desu-yo.

シン：本当ですか？
Shin：Honto desu-ka?

マイ：アニメグッズもたくさんありますよ。
Mai：Anime guzzu-mo takusan ari masu-yo.

シン：アニメグッズがほしいです。
Shin：Anime guzzu ga hoshii-desu.

Shin：What kind of place is Akihabara?

Mai：The place where anime is famous.

Shin：Really?

Mai：There is a lot of anime goods, too.

Shin：I'd like some anime goods.

Illustration by 小林オニキス
© Crypton Future Media, INC. www.piapro.net piapro

Let's try! Let's practice! Let's talk in Japanese! ▶日本語で会話してみよう！

 Challenge & Practice

Practice1 Ask and answer about the places listed.

N A：[　　　　　　　　]ってどんなところですか？
　　B：とてもすてきなところですよ。

R A: ...tte don'na tokoro desuka?
　　B: Totemo sutekina tokoro desu-yo.

E A: What kind of place is ...?
　　B: It's a very nice place.

N	R	E
秋葉原	Akihabara	Akihabara
ディズニーランド	Dizunî rando	Disney Land
原宿	Harajuku	Harajuku
新宿	Shinjuku	Shinjuku
沖縄	Okinawa	Okinawa
北海道	Hokkaidô	Hokkaidô

Options

Practice2 Let's try to say what you want by replacing with the listed words.

N [　　　　　　　　]がほしいです。

R ...ga hoshii desu.

E I want [　　　　].

N	R	E
水	mizu	water
メニュー	menyû	menu
フォーク	fôku	folk
もっと情報	motto jôhô	more information
地図	chizu	map

Options

101

6
Tell Your World

Tell Your World

This was produced for Google Chrome Japan for its campaign commercial. In this song, you can feel Miku singing her heart out delivering her message via Internet as a VOCALOID. Many Japanese fans describe this song as heart-rending. You can learn useful Japanese expressions to communicate in the cyber world.

▶ Japanese ［ 日本語 ］

作詞 kz
作曲 kz
唄 初音ミク

形のない気持ち忘れないように

決まりきった レイアウトを消した

ふと口ずさんだフレーズを掴まえて

胸に秘めた言葉乗せ 空に解き放つの

君に伝えたいことが 君に届けたいことが ■ ── Look at page 110.

たくさんの点は線になって 遠く彼方へと響く

君に伝えたい言葉 君に届けたい音が

いくつもの線は円になって 全て繋げてく

どこにだって

真っ白に澄んだ光は君のよう

かざした手の隙間を伝う声が

ふと動いた指先刻むリズムに

ありったけの言葉乗せ空に解き放つの

君に伝えたいことが 君に届けたいことが

Introduction ▶ 曲紹介

Google claims that "the web is simply just part of your life....The web is what you make of it when launching their new web browser "Chrome". The producer of the CM in Japan had no hesitation in using Hatsune Miku to represent "communication via Web". The CM theme song, "Tell Your World" was composed especially for the campaign.

SONOCA ▶ TRACK-6

たくさんの点は線になって 遠く彼方まで穿つ

君に伝えたい言葉 君に届けたい音が
いくつもの線は円になって 全て繋げてく
どこにだって

奏でていた 変わらない日々を疑わずに
朝は誰かがくれるものだと思っていた
一瞬でも信じた音
景色を揺らすの
教えてよ君だけの世界

君が伝えたいことは 君が届けたいことは
たくさんの点は線になって
遠く彼方へと響く
君が伝えたい言葉 君が届けたい音は
いくつもの線は円になって 全て繋げてく
どこにだって

Illustration by mebae
© Crypton Future Media, INC. www.piapro.net
©2011 mebae/ Kaikai Kiki Co., Ltd. All Rights Reserved.
©FANTASISTAUTAMARO ALL RIGHTS RESERVED.

Tell Your World

Roma-ji ▶

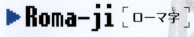

Sakushi	kz
Sakkyoku	kz
Uta	Hatsune Miku

Katachi-no nai kimochi wasure-nai yô-ni
Kimari-kitta rei'a'uto-o keshi-ta
Futo kuchi-zusa-nda furêzu-o tsukamae-te
Mune-ni hime-ta kotoba nosé sora-ni toki-hanatsu-no

Kimi-ni tsuta'e-ta'i koto-ga kimi-ni todoke-ta'i koto-ga
Takusan-no ten-wa sen-ni natte tôku kanata-e-to hibiku
Kimi-ni tsuta'e-ta'i kotoba kimi-ni todoke-ta'i oto-ga
Ikutsumono sen-wa en-ni natte subete tsunagete-ku
Dokoni-datte

Masshiro-ni sunda hikari-wa kimi-no yô
Kazashita te-no sukima-o tsutau koe-ga
Futo ugoita yubisaki kizamu rizumu-ni
Arittake-no kotoba nosé sora-ni toki-hanatsu-no

Kimi-ni tsuta'e-ta'i koto-ga kimi-ni todoke-ta'i koto-ga
Takusan-no ten-wa sen-ni natte tôku kanata-made ugatsu

Introduction ▶ 曲紹介

▶ Tell Your World

Kimi-ni tsuta'e-ta'i kotoba kimi-ni todoke-ta'i oto-ga

Ikutsumono sen-wa en-ni natte subete tsunagette-ku

Dokoni-datte

Kanadete-ita kawara-nai hibi-o utagawazu-ni

Asa-wa dareka-ga kureru mono-dato omotte-ita

Isshundemo shinjita oto

Keshiki-o yurasu-no

Oshiete-yo kimi-dake-no sekai

Kimi-ga tsuta'e-tai koto-wa kimi-ga todoke-tai koto-wa

Takusan'no ten-wa sen-ni natte

Tôku kanata-e-to hibiku

Kimi-ga tsuta'e-ta'i kotoba kimi-ga todoke-tai oto-wa

Ikutsumono sen-wa en-ni natte subete tsunagete-ku

Dokoni-datte

Translation ▶

▶ Translation [英訳]

- Words: kz
- Music: kz
- Translation: Water Knee
- Vocal: Hatsune Miku

The shapeless feelings deep that I possess to cherish forever
I just deleted the templates in my mind to clear my heart
I caught this little phrase that flew by and put it inside my heart
and put my intimate words to sing and shot it out to break through the sky

It's all the things to share and bare with your heart
It's all the things to shout and send to your heart
then all the dots combine into one line and they echo faraway across the distance

It's all the words to share and bear with your heart
It's all the notes to shout and send to your heart
Then all the lines combine into a circle
Comes down to one to tell your world it's here and everywhere

The crystal clear light that fills the air it always resembles you
Voices slipping through the fingers that I held toward the light
I felt this rhythm through my fingers moving and it came suddenly grasping
all the words I could find and shot it out to break through the sky

Introduction ▶ 曲紹介

▶ Tell Your World

It's all the things to share and bare with your heart
It's all the things to shout and send to your heart

Then all the dot combine into one line and
They sing through out the sky beyond the distance

It's all the words to share and bear with your heart
It's all the notes to shout and send to your heart
Then all the lines combine into a circle
Comes down to one to tell your world it's here and everywhere

Never doubted the days the sound that I played
I always thought the morning light
It was such an easy gift that will come and simply pour and rain on me
But still the sound that came and made me believe
It would shake my atmosphere
Tell Your World today the sound inside within your heart

It's all the things to share and bare with your heart
It's all the things to shout and send to your heart then all the dots combine
into one line and they echo faraway across the distance

It's all the words to share and bear with your heart
It's all the notes to shout and send to your heart
Then all the lines combine into a circle
Comes down to one to tell your world it's here and everywhere

109

Tell Your World

Context and Japanese Culture

文脈と日本の文化
Bunmyaku to Nihon no Bunka

The song expresses the Vocaloid's perspective of the Internet, connecting dots and lines, carrying messages through the sky. It resonates deeply with Japanese traditional culture.

Internet communication (インターネットコミュニケーション)

▶ In this song...

N	君に	伝えたい	こと
R	kimi-ni	tuta'e-ta'i	koto
E	to you	want to tell	thing(s)
M	The things I want to tell you		

Context and Japanese Culture ▶ 文脈と日本の文化

▶ Analysis

Internet communication online in Japan

This song touched so many fans' hearts by describing what you can do via the Internet. The app "LINE" is the main online communication tool in Japan while 2ch is still a very popular anonymous BBS.

People use different names and characters in the cyber world. In a sense, it means we have created a different world from offline.

Hatsune Miku and other Vocaloids are another online tool to publish your message to the world of all the things you want to "tell".

Key words 穿つ / ugatsu/

"ugatsu" is not used in everyday situations but survived only in the old saying, 点滴石を穿つ, meaning constant water dropping and drilling into the stone. "ugatsu" is a verb meaning "cut through", excavate (a tunnel) through, dig (to make a hole) or pierce. Selecting the word in this song makes us feel the millions of points(us) gather, piercing through the sky to reach far away.

Tips Miku can "tell your world" via Internet

A phrase just comes to mind, or you just hum a melody... it could make you a composer or lyric writer.You can do it with a vocaloid without a human singer, and you can tell "your world" online. All the dots are connected and online in the sky, and you can reach faraway.

Tell Your World

▶ Let's try! Let's practice! Let's talk in Japanese!

日本語で会話してみよう！

Nihongo de kaiwa Shitemiyô!

From this song, Japanese expressions to request things and what you want to do can be learned.

▶基本構文

❶ 〜たい。

R [verb] + ta'i.

E I want to [verb] .

❷ 〜たいです。

R [verb] + ta'i-desu.

E I would like to [verb] .

Let's try! Let's practice! Let's talk in Japanese! ▶日本語で会話してみよう！

▶ Casual scene   ▶ SONOCA ▶ TRACK-19

きみ：おなかすいたなぁ。
R Kimi: Onaka suita-na.

You : :I'm hungry.

ミク：そうだね。
R Miku: So-dané.

Miku : Yeah.

きみ：ラーメン食べたい。
R Kimi: Ra-men tabe-ta'i.

You : I want to eat Ramen noodles.

ミク：いいね！どこ行く？
R Miku: Îne! doko iku?

Miku: : Good idea! Where shall we go?

きみ：渋谷に行きたいな。
R Kimi:Shibuya-ni iki-ta'i-na.

You : I want to go to Shibuya.

113

Tell Your World

▶Formal scene   ▷ SONOCA ▶ TRACK-20

マイ：おなかがすきました。
R Mai : Onaka-ga suki mashita.

Mai : I'm hungry.

シン：そうですね。
R Shin : So-desu-ne.

Shin : Yeah.

マイ：ラーメンが食べたいです。
R Mai : Ramen-ga tabe-ta'i-desu.

Mai : I'd like to have Ramen noodles.

シン：いいですね！
　　　どこに行きましょうか？
R Shin : Î-desu-ne! doko-ni ikimasho-ka?

Shin : Good idea!
　　　Where shall we go?

マイ：渋谷に行きたいですね。
R Mai : Shibuya-ni ikita'i-desu-ne.

Mai : I'd like to go to Shibuya.

114

Let's try! Let's practice! Let's talk in Japanese! ▶日本語で会話してみよう!

Challenge & Practice

Practice 1 Select a verb from the options and tell what you want to do.

〜たいです。

R [verb] ta'i-desu.

E I want [verb].

Options

	dictionary form		masu-form	
❶	みる	R miru E see	み (ます)	R mi-masu E see
❷	のむ	R nomu E drink	のみ (ます)	R nomi-masu E drink

Practice 2 Select a noun and a verb from the options and tell what you want to do.

○○が〜たいです。

R [noun] -ga [verb] ta'i-desu.

E I would like to [verb].

	N	R	E
❸	お寿司	o-sushi	(honorific prefix: o + sushi)
❹	歌舞伎	kabuki	kabuki play
❺	水	mizu	water

	N	R	E (masu-form)
	食べる	taberu	tabe-
	見る	miru	mi-
	のむ	nomu	nomi-

Model Answer

Practice 1
❶ みたい   R mitai   ❷ のみたい   R nomitai

Practice 2
❸ お寿司、食べたい R tabetai   ❹ 歌舞伎、見たい R mitai
❺ 水、のみたい R nomitai

115

7 リモコン
Rimokon

Rimokon ▶リモコン

Rimokon

リモコン

Enjoy how Japanese rhymes in this pop melody with bouncy vocal. Feel the rythms of playing a video game, pushing buttons on the console, while understanding Rin and Len's wishes to become better and surpass other singers.

▶Japanese 「 日本語 」

作詞 じーざす
作曲 じーざす
唄 鏡音リン・レン

L R L R STOP & Dash & up & talk B B A B S(tart)

これが私をリモートコントロールする機械です
少し歪な形しておりますが、使えます

up side down Ａ Ｂ Ａ Ｂ Ｂ Ｂ Ａ Ｂ Ａ 左右
L R L R stop & Dash & up & talk 異常ナシ

もうちょっとで外に出られるのにな
どうやってもうまくいかね ◀━━━━━ Look at page 130.
まだ まだ 足りない !(Fooooooooo!!!)

座る 座る (oh)　sit down please(yeah!) フィードバックに体預けて
廻る 廻る (oh)　turn it around(yeah!) うなりをあげてモーター状態
踊る 踊る (oh)　dancin'night(yeah!) マッシュアップでもれなくアガる
声を (Fooooooooo!!!) あげて (oh) singin'now(yeah!) あの子よりもうまく歌いたい

118

Introduction ▶曲紹介

This song was produced to allow various interpretations.
Composed by Jizasu P who is a member of Wonderful★opportunity! (or Won-Opo in short),who mainly produce for Kagamine Rin & Len. Rimokon is the twelfth original song by Jizasu P with Taiwanese illustrator, Glider.
The song has reached over 1 million views in September 2012.

これがボクをリモートで操縦できる機械です
説明書は紛失しておりますが使えます

up side down Ａ Ｂ Ａ Ｂ Ｂ Ａ Ｂ Ａ 右 左
Ｌ Ｒ Ｌ Ｒ stop & dash & up & talk 異常ナシ

からかってるみたいないつもの顔 (余裕でしょ？)
今日はかなり本気だぜ
ほら すぐ キメるぜ

座る 座る (oh)　sit down please (yeah!) トークバックを頭に挿して
廻る 廻る (oh)　turn it around(yeah!) ちょっと待ってスタンバイ状態
踊る 踊る (oh)　dancin'night(yeah!) ジャストフィットなリズムを出して
唸り (aohhhh!!!) あげる (oh) singin'now(yeah!) アイツよりも高く歌いたい

Rimokon ▶リモコン

Japanese ▶

惚れた晴れたの七色侍

洗いざらい主張する存在

思い違いが透けてる塩梅

怖いくらいの wktk 状態 ◀━━━━━━━━ Look at page 130.

気にしないのがアナタのポリシー？

悩んでいてもお腹は減るし

なんだかんだで世間はヘルシー

お気を確かにぬるま湯男子ぃ！ぃぃぃぃぃぃぃぃぃぃぃぃぃぃぃぃぃぃ

(uhhh...wow!!)

もうちょっとでスキマ埋まるのにな (埋まるのに)

どうやってもうまくいかね

ああ、もう時間が足りない！

Introduction ▶曲紹介

▶リモコン

座る 座る (oh)　sit down please(yeah!) フィードバックに体預けて
廻る 廻る (oh)　turn it around(yeah!) 唸りをあげて モーター状態
踊る 踊る (oh) dancin'night(yeah!) マッシュアップでもれなくアガる!
声を (Foooooooo!!!) あげて (oh) singin'now(yeah!) あの子みたいなヒトになりたい

座る 座る sit down please

(up side down A B A B B A B A A B A B)

廻る 廻る turn it around

(L R L R stop & dash & L R L R stop & dash &)

踊る 踊る dancin'night

(up side down A B A B B A B A A B A B)

声をあげて singin'now

(L R L R stop & dash & L R L R B A B A)

あの子みたいなヒトになりたい

Rimokon ▶リモコン

Roma-ji ▶

▶▶ Roma-ji 「ローマ字」

Sakushi▶ Jizasu
Sakkyoku▶ Jizasu
Uta▶ Kagamine Rin/Len

L R L R STOP & Dash & UP & TALK B B A B S(tart)

Kore-ga watashi-o rimôto kontorôru suru kika'i-desu
Sukoshi ibitsu-na katachi shite-ori-masu-ga, tsuka'e-masu

up side down A B A B B A B A hidari migi
L R L R stop & Dash & up & talk ijô nashi

Mô chotto-de soto-ni dera-reru-noni-na
Dô yatte-mo umaku ika-ne
Mada mada tari-n'ai (Foooooooo!!!)

Suwaru suwaru (oh) sit down please (yeah!)
Fîdo bakku-ni karada azuke-te
Meguru meguru (oh) turn it around (yeah!)
Unari-wo age-te môtâ jôtai
Odoru odoru (oh) dancin'night (yeah!)
Masshu appu-de morenaku agaru
Koe-o (Foooooooo!!!) age-te (oh) singin'now (yeah!)
Ano ko-yori-mo umaku utai-tai

Introduction ▶曲紹介

▶ Rimokon

Kore-ga boku-o remôto-de sôj-u dekiru kika'i-desu

Setsume'isho-wa funshitsu-shite-ori-masu-ga tsuka'e-masu

up side down A B A B B A B A migi hidari

L R L R stop & dash & up & talk ijô nashi

Karaka-tteru mitai-na itsumo-no ka'o(Yoyû de-sho?)

Kyo-wa kanari honki-da-ze?

Hora sugu kimeru-ze

Suwaru suwaru (oh) sit down please (yeah!)

Tôku bakku-wo atama-ni sashi-te

Meguru meguru (oh) turn it around (yeah!)

Chotto ma-tte, sutanba'i jôtai

Odoru odoru (oh) dancin'night (yeah!)

Jasuto fitto-na rizumu-o dashi-te

Unari (aohhhh!!!) ageru (oh) singin'now (yeah!)

Aitsu-yori-mo takaku uta'i-ta'i

Rimokon ▶ リモコン

Roma-ji ▶

Horeta hareta-no nanairo zamura'i

Arizarai shucho-suru sonzai

Omo'ichiga'i-ga sukete-ru anba'i

Kowa'i-kura'i-no waku-tekajôta'i

Ki-ni shi-na'i-no-ga anata-no porishî?

Nayan-de ite-mo onaka-wa heru-shi

Nanda kanda-de seken-wa herushî

Oki-o tashika-ni nurumayu danshi-iiiiiiiiii (uhhhh...wow!!)

Mô chotto-de sukima umaru-no-ni-na (umaru-no-ni)

Dô yatte-mo umaku ika-né

Ah mô jikan-ga tari-na'i!

Introduction ▶ 曲紹介

▶ Rimokon

Suwaru suwaru (oh) sit down please (yeah!)

Fîdo bakku-ni karada azuke-te

Meguru meguru (oh) turn it around (yeah!)

Unari-o age-te môtâ jôta'i

Odoru odoru (oh) dancin'night (yeah!)

Masshu appu-de more-naku agaru!

Koe'-o (Fooooooooo!!!) age-té (oh) sing in'now (yeah!)

Ano ko mita'i-na hito-ni nari-ta'i

Suwaru suwaru sit down please

(up side down A B A B B A B A A B A B)

Meguru meguru turn it around

(L R L R stop & dash & L R L R stop & dash &)

Odoru odoru dancin'night

(up side down A B A B B A B A A B A B)

Koe-o age-te singin'now

(L R L R stop & dash & L R L R B A B A)

Ano ko mita'i-na hito-ni nari-ta'i

Rimokon ▶リモコン

Translation ▶

▶Translation 　[英訳]

Words ▶ Jizasu
Music ▶ Jizasu
Vocal ▶ Kagamine Rin/Len

L R L R STOP & Dash & up & talk B B A B S(tart)

This is the remote which remotely controls me
The shape is a bit rickety, but it works OK

up side down A B A B B A B A left right
L R L R stop & Dash & up & talk　Normal operation

I can almost break out of this
but I can't
I need more to work on, Hooooooooooooo

Sit, sit, oh sit down, please, yeah!　Leaning back to the feed back
Turn, turn, oh turn it around, yeah!　whirring like a motor
Dance, dance, dancing night, yeah!　Mashup ! Total Mashup !
Sing louder, singing now, yeah!　I want to sing better than them

Introduction ▶ 曲紹介

▶ Rimokon

This is a tool which can remotely control me

No manual attached, but it works OK

up side down A B A B B B A B A right left

L R L R stop & dash & up & talk Normal operation

The usual teasing face...

I'm serious today, y'know?

Look, I'll get it, now!

Sit, sit, sit down, please, yeah! Putting the Talk-back on my head

Turn, turn, turn it around, yeah! Wait, I'm in stand-by mode

Dance, dance, dancing night, yeah! Using the rythmes that just fit

Roar, ahhhhhh, up! oh Singin'now, yeah! I want to sing in higher

pitch than them

Rimokon ▶ リモコン

Translation ▶

Rainbow coloured Samurai deep in love

Persisting in everything to the full

Transparent misunderstanding, just like

wktk (excited) to fear

No worry is your policy?

Worried but hungry, you see

Whatever you say, the world is healthy

Attention, boys with tepid hearts

uhhhh.. WOW!!!

I'm just about filling the gaps.

It doesn't go well whatever I do.

Ah, running out of time

Sit, sit, sit down, please, yeah! Leaning on the feedback

Turn, turn, turn it around, yeah! Roaring like an engine gunning

Dance, dance, dancing night, yeah! Mashup! Total Mashup!

Sing louder! oh singing now yeah! I want to be a hit like them

Introduction ▶曲紹介

▶ Rimokon

Sit, sit sit down, please

(up side down A B A B B A B A A B A B)

Turn, turn, turn it around

(L R L R stop & dash & L R L R stop & dash &)

Dance, dance, dancin'night

(up side down A B A B B A B A A B A B)

Sing louder! singin'now

(L R L R stop & dash & L R L R stop & dash &)

I want to be a hit like them

Illustration by グライダー
© Crypton Future Media, INC. www.piapro.net piapro

Context and Japanese Culture

文脈と日本の文化
Bunmyaku to Nihon no Bunka

Introducing slang and young people's way of talking.

Teen slang (若者言葉)

▶ In this song...

N	どうやっても	うまく	いかね。
R	dô yatte-mo	umaku	ika-ne.
E	whatever [S] do	well	it does not go
M	whatever [S] do, it does not go well			

Slang on the Internet (ネットスラング)

▶ In this song...

N	w k t k	状態
R	wakuteka	jôtai
E	excited-grossy	state
M	excited-grossy ||

Context and Japanese Culture ▶ 文脈と日本の文化

▶ Analysis

Teen slang "- né" for "nai"

"-ne" is the short form of the denial suffix "nai ない". It's quite a recent usage by young people in certain contexts, shortening from "nai".
/ne/ → ねえ /nee/ to /ne/ and has been fashionable in the casual scenes.

そうじゃね？(so ja ne?) It's so, isn't it?
おいしくね？(oishiku-ne?) Tasty, isn't it?
よくね？(yoku ne?) Good, isn't it?"

It works like a tag question.

> **Key words** **WKTK/excited-glossy/**
>
> wktk is abbreviation of waku-waku, teka-teka, used by *2ch users (Waku-waku is an onomatopoeia meaning to get excited, to look forward to something. Teka-teka is also an onomatopoeia which describes being glossy.) Thus wktk describes somebody so excitedly looking forward to something that the skin is glossy with sweat.

*2ch: 2 channel was one of the most popular text board in Japan. With more than 1,000 active boards, it's been influential in the society. Now rebranded as 5ch(as of 2018).

Tips **L,R, up and down**

L,R, up, down as on the game console. In the video, Rin has a game console while Len has a TV remote, but both tools actually control them. The rhythm of the words is more important than consistent meaning, as always in game playing. As you sing, imagine you are playing a fighting game, or Hatsune Miku Project Diva which contains this song.

Rimokon ▶リモコン

▶ Let's try! Let's practice! Let's talk in Japanese!

日本語で会話してみよう！
Nihongo de kaiwa shitemiyô!

Let's practice one of the Japanese verb conjugation forms: denial ("-nai" form) of basic verbs. This will help you a lot to enjoy conversation in various scenes!

▶ 基本構文1

① 座る→座らない　(dictionary form)

R Suwaru → suwara-na'i
E Sit (down) → sit (down) ‐ not
M do not sit (down)

② 座ります→座りません　(polite form)

R Suwari-masu → suwari-masen
E Sit (down)+ [honorific：masu] → sit (down) ‐ not
M do not sit (down)

Let's try! Let's practice! Let's talk in Japanese! ▶日本語で会話してみよう！

▶ Casual scene SONOCA ▶ TRACK-21

ミク：ここ、座る？
R Miku:Koko suwaru?

Miku：Will you sit here?

きみ：ううん、いい。座らない。
R Kimi: Ûn, î. suwara-nai.

You：Noop. Thanks. I won't sit.

ミク：ほんと？じゃあ、じゃあ、これ、食べる？
R Miku:Honto? Jâ,jâ kore taberu?

Miku：Really? Then, will you eat this?

きみ：どうしよう。
R Kimi:Dô shi-yô.

You：What will I do?

ミク：食べないの？
R Miku:Tabe-nai-no?

Miku：You won't eat?

きみ：やっぱり、食べる！
R Kimi:Yappari taberu!

You：Well, I will!

133

Rimokon ▶リモコン

▶ Formal scene

▶ SONOCA ▶ TRACK-22

マイ：ここ、座りますか？

R Mai:Koko suwari-masu-ka?

Mai：Would you sit here?

シン：いいえ、結構です。
　　　座りません。

R Shin: Îe, kekko-desu.
　　　　Suwari-masen.

Shin：No, thank you. I won't.

マイ：そうですか？じゃあ、これ、
　　　召し上がりますか？

R Mai:So-desu-ka? Jâ, kore
　　　meshiagari-masu-ka?

Mai：Is that so? Well, would
　　　you like to eat this?

シン：どうしましょう。

R Shin: Dô shi-mashô.

Shin：Not sure.
　　　(what shall I do?)

マイ：召し上がりませんか？

R Mai:Meshiagari-masen-ka?

Mai：Won't you eat?

シン：やっぱり、いただきます。

R Shin: Yappari
　　　itadaki-masu.

Shin：Well, I'd like to eat.

Let's try! Let's practice! Let's talk in Japanese! ▶ 日本語で会話してみよう！

Challenge & Practice

Let's try to make a "nai-form" from the dictionary form.

	dictionary form	nai-form	te-form	masu-form
Group I	すわる (suwa-ru) :sit	① [　　　　] ない	すわって	すわります
	まわる (mawa-ru) :turn	② [　　　　] ない	まわって	まわります
	おどる (odo-ru) :dance	③ [　　　　] ない	おどって	おどります
	のむ (no-mu) :drink	④ [　　　　] ない	のんで	のみます
	きる (ki-ru) :cut	⑤ [　　　　] ない	きって	きります
Group II	おきる (oki-ru) :get up	⑥ [　　　　] ない	おきて	おきます
	たべる (tabe-ru) :eat	⑦ [　　　　] ない	たべて	たべます
Group III	する (su-ru) :do	⑧ [　　　　] ない	して	します
	くる (ku-ru) :come	⑨ [　　　　] ない	きて	きます

Answer

①すわらない (suwara-nai)　②まわらない (mawara-nai)　③おどらない (odora-nai)
④のまない (noma-nai)　⑤きらない (kira-nai)　⑥おきない (oki-nai)　⑦たべない (tabe-nai)
⑧しない (shi-nai)　⑨こない (ko-nai)

8

微風ドライブ
そよかぜ
Soyokaze Drive

Soyokaze Drive 微風ドライブ

The producer 40mP created this song to make a fresh and summery image of waves lapping the beach, of cycling, of the buzz of cicadas and summer rain; typical sounds of the summer in Japan. With this song, you will really feel the Japanese summer!

▶ Japanese [日本語]

作詞 40mP
作曲 40mP
唄 初音ミク

LR のスピーカー　響き渡るスネア
駆け抜けた砂浜　重なり合うリズム

聴き慣れたサウンド　ありきたりなコード
打ち寄せるさざ波　鳴り止まないディレイ

窓から差し込む陽射しが
頭上に浮かぶ雲が
ハーモニーを奏で合って
イントロが終わる頃

微風のような君の歌声が街を染めて
浮かない顔した僕の髪を揺らして
また夏が来る

> Look at page 144.

Introduction ▶曲紹介

This song was sold only for two months in the summer in 2016 by a Japanese company, Banpresto as a number lottery.Ichiban Kuji with various character goods as prizes. This song was created for the summer campaign with the collaboration of Ichiban Kuji and SONOCA (a illustration/collectible card download password which allowed the user to download a song). It became popular for Miku's fresh voice and visual, created by popular illustrators, En Morikura, pemu and Kamogawa.

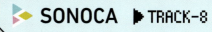

SONOCA ▶ TRACK-8

壊れかけのアンプ　誤魔化したディストーション
サビついた自転車　胸を焦がすノイズ

上げ過ぎたボリューム　赤く光るピーク
通り過ぎる時間　夏はフェードアウト

予報外れの通り雨が
乾いた蝉の声が
ハーモニーを奏で合って
季節が移ろう頃

Illustration by 賀茂川
© Crypton Future Media, INC. www.piapro.net

朝焼けのような君の歌声が海を染めて
一筋の涙　僕の頬を照らしてゆく

微風のような君の歌声が街を染めて
鮮やかな季節　いつも僕の心に　澄み渡る青空に
また夏が来る

微風が僕を包んで　いくつもの音を奏でるよ
悲しみさえも追い越すスピードで
歌声届けてくれた

Roma-ji

▶Roma-ji [ローマ字]

Sakushi: 40mP
Sakkyoku: 40mP
Uta: Hatsune Miku

Illustration by 森倉円
© Crypton Future Media, INC. www.piapro.net piapro

LR-no spîkâ hibiki-wataru sune'a
Kake-nuketa sunahama, kasanari-au rizumu

Kiki-nareta saundo arikitari-na kôdo
Uchi-yoseru sazanami nari-yama-nai dire'i

Mado-kara sashi-komu hizashi-ga
Zujô-ni ukabu kumo-ga
Hâmonî-o kanade-atte
Intoro-ga owaru koro

Soyokaze-no-yôna kimi-no utagoe-ga machi-o some-te
Uka-nai kao-shita boku-no kami-o yurashi-te
Mata natsu-ga kuru

Introduction ▶ 曲紹介

▶ Soyokaze drive

Kowarekake-no ampu gomakashi-ta disutôshon

Sabi-tsui-ta jitensha mune-o kogasu noizu

Age-sugita boryûmu akaku hikaru pîku

Tôri-sugiru jikan natsu-wa fêdo a'uto

Yohô-hazure-no tôri-amé-ga

Kawai-ta semi-no koe-ga

Hâmonî-o kanade-a-tte

Kisetsu-ga utsuro'u koro

Asayake-no-yôna kimi-no utagoe-ga umi-o some-te

Hitosuji-no namida boku-no hô-o terashi-te yuku

Soyokaze-no-yôna kimi-no utagoe-ga machi-o some-te

Azayaka-na kisetsu itsumo boku-no kokoro-ni sumi-wataru aozora-ni

Mata natsu-ga kuru

Soyokaze-ga boku-o tsutsun-de ikutsumo-no oto-o kanaderu-yo

Kanashimi-sae-mo o'ikosu spîdo-de

Utagoe todoke-te kure-ta

Translation

▶ Translation [英訳]

- Words: 40mP
- Music: 40mP
- Vocal: Hatsune Miku

Echoing snares From the Speakers L&R, Running on the beach, Overlapping rythms,

Sounds we got used to listening to, ordinary codes,
Waves crash ashore, while music brings delayed sounds one after another,

Sunlight through the window
Clouds above
Meeting in harmony
to end the intro, then...

Your voice like a breeze filling the town
Tousling my hair over my sulky face
A summer is coming...

Illustration by pemu
© Crypton Future Media, INC. www.piapro.net

Introduction ▶ 曲紹介

▶ Soyokaze drive

Nearly broken amp, cheated distortion
Rusty bicycle, heart-breaking noise

Volume too loud, Peak showing red
Time passing, the summer fading out

Unexpected rain shower, and
Cicadas crying out
create the harmony
of the changing season, then...

Your voice like the glow of the morning sky colouring the sea,
Lights the track of a tear on my cheek

Your voice like a breeze filling the town
A bright season, a clear blue sky colours my mind
Another summer is coming...

A breeze wraps around me and plays its melody
Its speed chases away the sadness and
carries your voice to me...

Soyokaze drive ▶微風ドライブ

▶ Context and Japanese Culture

文脈と日本の文化

Bunmyaku to Nihon no Bunka

Talking about Japanese summer and related nuance and culture.

Breeze (微風)

▶ In this song...

N	微風のような	君の	歌声
R	soyokaze-no-yôna	kimi-no	utago'e
E	breeze-like	your	singing voice
M	your singing voice like breeze		

Early summer (初夏)

▶ In this song...

N	また	夏が	来る
R	mata	natsu-ga	kuru
E	Another	summer	is coming
M	Another summer is coming		

144

Context and Japanese Culture ▶ 文脈と日本の文化

▶ Analysis

24 seasons and early summer in Japan

How many seasons are there in Japan? If you ask Japanese they would say "four", but actually, we used to separate the year into 24 seasons. Many are not used every day but "shunbun" and "shûbun" (equinoxes in spring and autumn), "toji" (around 20 December when the chill becomes severe) are heard from weather news regularly. This song was released in "sho-ka 初夏", early summer in Japan to bring a summer mood and suggest sentimental memories of a past summer breeze.

Key words 微風 /Soyokaze/

The song title "Soyokaze" written 微風 in Japanese. With changing, and often unpredictable climate, we have many words for wind.

台風 (Taifû): Typhoon

　　　嵐 (Arashi): storm

つむじ風・旋風 (Tsumuji kaze): tornado

はやて・疾風 (Hayate): sudden gale

ビル風 (Biru kaze): Strong winds
　　　　　around high
　　　　　buildings

吹雪 (fubuki): snowstorm

夜風 (Yokaze): night breeze

こがらし・凩・木枯し (Kogarashi):
　strong winter wind

北風・きたかぜ・
朔風 (Kita kaze) ： North wind

春風 (Haru kaze): spring wind

Tips **The Image of Summer in Japan**

The Japanese summer is long and full of senses, sounds, images and experiences such as summer camps, long journeys, festivals, fireworks and first love. Refreshing watermelon, cold noodles, barley tea, the gentle sound of wind chimes, the cool feel of a yukata also bring us nostalgia of summer.

Soyokaze drive ▶ 微風ドライブ

▶ Let's try! Let's practice! Let's talk in Japanese!

日本語で会話してみよう！

Nihongo de kaiwa shitemiyô!

You can learn auxiliary verbs which show and example of the speaker's guessing here. Let's see the difference between "mita'ina" and "yôna" with the conversations.

▶ 基本構文

❶ ～のような／～みたいな

R [Noun] + no-yôna + (Noun)

　[Noun] + mita'ina + (Noun)

E (Noun) like [Noun], (Noun) such as [Noun]

Both are auxilary verbs which show an example of the speaker's guessing. While "mita'ina" is used in the casual speech, "yôna" is for written texts or formal conversation.

146

Let's try! Let's practice! Let's talk in Japanese! ▶ 日本語で会話してみよう！

▶ Casual scene   SONOCA ▶ TRACK-23

きみ：ねえ、ねえ、お好み焼きって何？
R Kimi:Nee, nee, okonomiyaki-tte nani?

You：Miku, what is Okonomiyaki?

ミク：ピザみたいな食べ物だよ。
R Miku:Piza mita'i-na tabemono dayo.

Miku：It's a dish like pizza.

きみ：へえ、じゃあ、すき焼きって何？
R Kimi:Hee, jaa, sukiyaki-tte nani?

You：OK, then, what is Sukiyaki?

ミク：うーんとね、牛肉のシチューみたいな感じかなぁ。
R Miku: Ûn-tone, gyûniku no shichû mita'i-na kanji kanâ.

Miku：Well… it's like beef stew, I think.

きみ：ふうん、おいしい？
R Kimi:Fuun, oishii?

You：Hmmm, is it tasty?

ミク：うん、すごくおいしいよ！
R Miku:Un, sugoku oishî yo!

Miku：Sure! it's so good.

Okonomiyaki

Sukiyaki

147

Soyokaze drive ▶微風ドライブ

▶Formal scene

SONOCA ▶ TRACK-24

マイ：すみません、お好み焼きって何ですか？

Ⓡ Mai:Sumimasen, okonomiyaki-
tte nann desu-ka?

Mai : Excuse me, what is
okonomiyaki?

シン：ピザのような食べ物です。

Ⓡ Shin:Piza no yô-na tabemono
desu.

Shin : It's a dish like pizza.

マイ：なるほど。では、すき焼きって何ですか？

Ⓡ Mai:Naruhodo, Dewa,
sukiyaki-tte nann desu-ka?

Mai : I see, then, what is
sukiyaki?

シン：そうですね、牛肉のシチューの
ようなものです。

Ⓡ Shin:Soudesu-ne, gyûniku no
shichû no yô-na mono desu.

Shin : Well, it's like beef stew.

マイ：そうですか。おいしいですか？

Ⓡ Mai:Soudesu ka.
Oishii desu ka?

Mai : I see. Is it tasty?

シン：はい、とてもおいしいですよ！

Ⓡ Shin:Hai, totemo oishî desu-yo!

Shin : Yes, it's very tasty.

Let's try! Let's practice! Let's talk in Japanese! ▶日本語で会話してみよう！

✏ Challenge & Practice

Practice ▶ Connect (A), (B) and (C) with either "yôna" or "mita'ina" to make a phrase.

（ A ）	のように	（ B ）	（ C ）

Example ▶

N	雪	のように	白い	肌
R	yuki	no-yôni	shiroi	hada
E	snow	like	white	skin
M	white skin like snow			

Options ▶

(A)	(B)	(C)
鬼 (oni: demon)	熱い (atsui: hot)	先生 (sensei: teacher)
火 (hi: fire)	怖い (kowai: scaring)	気持ち (kimochi: feeling)

Challenge ▶ Choose a word from the option (D) and fill in the brackets.

キミの	声は	（ D ）	みたいだね。

Example ▶

R	kimi-no	ko'e-wa	kodomo	mita'i dane.
E	Your	voice	children	is like
M	Your voice is like children.			

Options ▶ (D) 天使 (tenshi：angel), 小鳥 (kotori：small bird), ミク (Miku)

Model Answer

Practice ❶ (A) 鬼 R oni (B) 怖い R kowai (C) 先生 R sensei

❷ (A) 火 R hi (B) 熱い R atsui (C) 気持ち R kimochi

Challenge ❶キミの声は (D) 天使 R tenishi　みたいだね。

❷キミの声は (D) 小鳥 R kotori　みたいだね。

❸キミの声は (D) ミク R Miku　みたいだね。

9
桜ノ雨
Sakura no ame

Sakura no ame ▶桜ノ雨

Sakura no ame

桜ノ雨

This song became very popular at school graduation ceremonies in Japan. As you sing, imagine the cherry blossoms petals floating down like rain. In Japan, the image is a symbol of departure, farewell and separation.

▶Japanese [日本語]

作詞 ▶ halyosy
作曲 ▶ halyosy
唄 ▶ 初音ミク

それぞれの場所へ旅立っても

友達だ

聞くまでもないじゃん

十人十色に輝いた日々が

胸張れと背中押す

土埃上げ競った校庭

窮屈で着くずした制服

机の上に書いた落書き

どれもこれも僕らの証

白紙の答辞には伝えきれない

思い出の数だけ涙が滲む

幼くて傷つけもした

僕らは少しくらい

大人になれたのかな

> Look at page 164.

Introduction ▶曲紹介

This song was originally released by Haruyoshi Mori a.k.a 'halyosy', in "Niko Niko Dōga" in February, 2008.The song was novelized as "Sakura no Ame," in 2012, then made to a movie (English Title "Cherry Blossom Memories") .

教室の窓から桜ノ雨

ふわりてのひら

心に寄せた

みんな集めて出来た花束を

空に放とう

忘れないで

今はまだ小さな花弁だとしても

僕らはひとりじゃない

Illustration by iXima

Sakura no ame ▶桜ノ雨

Japanese ▶

下駄箱で見つけた恋の実

廊下で零した不平不満

屋上で手繰り描いた未来図

どれもこれも僕らの証

卒業証書には書いてないけど

人を信じ人を愛して学んだ

泣き

笑い

喜び

怒り

僕らみたいに青く

青く晴れ渡る空

教室の窓から桜ノ虹

ゆめのひとひら

胸奮わせた

出会いの為の別れと信じて

手を振り返そう

忘れないで

いつかまた大きな花弁を咲かせ

僕らはここで逢おう

154

Introduction ▶ 曲紹介

桜ノ雨

幾千の学び舎の中で
僕らが巡り逢えた奇跡
幾つ歳をとっても変わらないで
その優しい笑顔

教室の窓から桜ノ雨
ふわりてのひら
心に寄せた
みんな集めて出来た花束を
空に放とう

忘れないで
今はまだ小さな花弁だとしても
僕らはひとりじゃない

いつかまた大きな花弁を咲かせ
僕らはここで逢おう

Illustration by iXima
© Crypton Future Media, INC. www.piapro.net

Roma-ji

▶Roma-ji [ローマ字]

Sakushi halyosy
Sakkyoku halyosy
Uta Hatsune Miku

Sorezore-no basho-e tabida-ttemo

Tomodachi-da

Kiku-madé-mo-nai-jan

Jûnin' toiro-ni

Kagayai-ta hibi-ga

Muné haré-to senaka osu

Tsuchi bokori age kiso-tta kōtei

Kyukutsu-de kikuzusi-ta seifuku

Tsukue-no ue-ni kai-ta rakugaki

Dore-mo kore-mo bokura-no akashi

Hakushi-no tōji-niwa tsutae kire-nai

Omoide-no kazu-dake namida-ga nijimu

Osanaku-te kizutsuke-mo shi-ta

Bokura-wa sukosi-kurai

Otona-ni nare-ta-no-kana

Introduction ▶ 曲紹介

▶ Sakura no ame

Kyoshitsu-no mado-kara sakura-no ame

Fuwari tenohira

Kokoro-ni yoseta

Min'na atsume-té deki-ta hanataba-wo

Sora-ni hanatou

Wasure-na'i-dé

Ima-wa mada chiisana hanabira-dato shi-temo

Bokura-wa hitori-ja-na'i

Sakura no ame ▶桜ノ雨

Roma-ji ▶

Getabako-de mitsuke-ta koi-no mi

Rôka-de koboshi-ta fuhei fuman

Okujô-de taguri egaita miraizu

Doremo koremo bokura-no akashi

Sotsugyo shosho-niwa kai-te-nai-kedo

Hito-o shinji hito-o aishi-te manan-da

Naki

Warai

Yorokobi

Ikari

Bokura-mita'i-ni aoku

Aoku harewataru sora

Kyoshitsu-no mado-kara sakura-no niji

Yume-no hitohira

Mune furuwaseta

De'ai-no tame-no wakare-to shinjite

Te-o furika'e-sô

Wasure-na'i-de

Itsuka mata ôkina hanabira-o sakase

Bokura-wa koko-de aô

Introduction 曲紹介

▶ Sakura no ame

Ikusen-no manabiya-no naka-de

Bokura-ga meguri aeta kiseki

Ikutsu toshi-o tottemo kawara-nai-de

Sono yasahii egao

Kyoshitsu-no mado-kara sakura-no ame

Fuwari tenohira

Kokoro-ni yoseta

Min'na atsume-te deki-ta hanataba-wo

Sora-ni hanatou

Wasure-na'i-de

Ima-wa mada chiisana hanabira-dato shi-temo

Bokura-wa hitori-ja-na'i

Itsuka mata ôkina hanabira-o sakase

Bokura-wa koko-de aô

Illustration by iXima
© Crypton Future Media, INC. www.piapro.net

Sakura no ame ▶桜ノ雨

Translation ▶

▶ Translation　［ 英訳 ］

Words　halyosy
Music　halyosy
Vocal　Hatsune Miku

We are all going to different places

But we're friends,

we don't even have to ask

Through those days each of us flourished

We can stand tall and be proud of ourselves

The school yard where we played in the dirt

Loosening our tight uniforms, here and there

The graffiti on the desks

Each of them witnesses that we were here

There is no message in the speech read from a blank paper

Tear drops as many as memories

We were young, we hurt each other

Are we mature enough now, I wonder?

Introduction ▶曲紹介

▶ Sakura no ame

A rain of Cherryblossom petals from the classroom windows

Gently landed on my palm,

Reaching my heart

I gathered them all to make a bouquet

And tossed it to the sky,

wishing forget me not

Small petals are we still

But we are not alone

Illustration by iXima
© Crypton Future Media, INC. www.piapro.net

Sakura no ame ▶桜ノ雨

Translation ▶

A seed of love found in a shoe box (*)

Grumbling in the hallway

On the rooftop, our hands draw our future plans

They are all our witnesses

It's not written in our diplomas,

but we learned how to trust and how to love

We cried,

We laughed;

Were happy,

Got angry

Just like us(*2), a blue, blue, clear sky unfolds above us

A rainbow of cherry blossoms through the school window

Brought a piece of dream to touch my heart

Believing its purpose was to send me to my next encounter, I waved

goodbye

 Wave back,

forget me not

Someday again, fully bloomed

We'll reunite here

A seed of love found in a shoe box (*)
Traditionally in Japan, love letters are stashed inside the getabako (shoe box) which is not so popular these days, but the custom still continues.
At school in Japan, students change to their in-house shoes in the morning and outside shoes are stored in their shoe box (no lock) at the entrance.

Just like us(*2), a blue, blue, clear sky unfolds above us.
Japanese colour "ao" could mean blue, blue-ish or green, and often refers to youth or springtime of life, e.g. "seishun"(青春) literally blue/green spring.

Introduction ▶ 曲紹介

▶ Sakura no ame

Out of thousands of schools,

it was a miracle we met here

However many years you add

Do not change it

your gentle smile

Cherryblossoms petals raining in

from the school windows

Gently landed on my palm, reaching my heart

I gathered them all to make a bouquet

And tossed it to the sky,

wishing forget me not

Small petals are we still

But we are not alone

Someday again, fully bloomed

We'll reunite here

Sakura no ame ▶桜ノ雨

▶ Context and Japanese Culture

文脈と日本の文化
Bunmyaku to Nihon no Bunka

This song contains many examples of Japanese school life. The school year begins and ends when the sakura is in bloom.

Graduation Ceremony (卒業)

▶ In this song...

N	白紙の	答辞には	伝えきれない
R	hakushi-no	tôji-niwa	tsuta'e kire-nai
E	blank paper	the speech read	not enough to tell
M	There is no message in the speech read from a blank paper		

N	思い出の	数だけ	涙が	滲む
R	omoide-no	kazu-dake	namida-ga	nijimu
E	of memories	as many as	tear	drops
M	tear drops as many as memories			

N	窮屈で	着くずした	制服
R	kyukutsu-de	ki-kuzushi-ta	seifuku
E	so tight	loosen	uniform
M	loosing our tight uniforms		

Context and Japanese Culture ▶ 文脈と日本の文化

▶ Analysis

School Days and Graduation Ceremonies in Japan

In Japan, graduation ceremonies are a solemn event. Many of them start with an opening address, and continue with the national anthem, presentation of the diplomas, followed by a number of speeches including a farewell address by younger students called 送辞 (souji). In reply to "souji", the graduating students give a 答辞 (touji). There's no word "graduation ceremony" in this song. Sakura implies it's the time of separation and departure while this "touji" clearly identifies the event.

Key words 制服 /uniform& uniformity/

There are so many "kawaii" uniforms for Japanese high schools. The uniform is one of the most important aspects when girls choose a school. Schools want the uniform to be worn conservatively, but students often try to individualize it by shortening the skirt, opening the collar, etc. In this song "kyukutsu-na (tight in size and also mentality)" and "kikuzusu(loosen up, relax) seifuku" indicate the strict insistence on uniformity in Japan's schools. At graduation, though, this strictness is a bitter-sweet memory.

Tips Rain of Sakura... the symbol of separation and graduation in Japan

Sakura petals fall like rain. Strong winds often arrive with spring, ending the cold weather, and scattering the sakura. Graduation ceremonies of Japanese schools are held in March when both academic and fiscal year end amidst a rain of sakura. Thus sakura connotes for Japanese memories, of schooldays and separation as well as the start of new life.

165

Sakura no ame ▶ 桜ノ雨

▶ Let's try! Let's practice! Let's talk in Japanese!

日本語で会話してみよう！

Nihongo de kaiwa shitemiyô!

From this song, more variations of Japanese such as connecting nouns and negative imperatives can be learned.

▶ 基本構文

❶ AのBから

R [(noun)A]-[particle: "no"] [(noun)B]-[particle: "kara"]

E [(noun)A] of [(noun)B] from

M from B of A

❷ 〜ないで

R [te-form]+na'i+[particle:de]

E [verb(te-form)]+[suffic:na'i (denial)]+[particle:de (connective)]

M Do not [verb]

Let's try! Let's practice! Let's talk in Japanese! ▶ 日本語で会話してみよう！

▶ Casual scene   SONOCA ▶ TRACK-25

ミク：どこから来たの？
® Miku: Doko-kara kita-no?

きみ：インドネシアのジャカルタから。
® Kimi: Indoneshia-no jakaruta-kara.

ミク：今度、一緒に、秋葉原に行こう。
® Miku: Kondo issho-ni Akihabara-ni ikou.

きみ：約束だよ。忘れないでね。
® Kimi: Yakusoku-dayo. wasure-na'i-dé-né.

Miku : Where are you from?

You : I'm from Jakarta in Indonesia.

Miku : Someday, let's go to Akihabara together!

You : It's a promise. Don't forget it!

167

▶ Formal scene　　　SONOCA ▶ TRACK-26

シン：どちらからいらっしゃいましたか？

R　Shin：Dochira-kara irassha'i mashita-ka?

Shin：Where are you from?

マイ：インドネシアのジャカルタからです。

R　Mai：Indoneshia-no jakaruta-kara desu.

Mai：I'm from Jakarta in Indonesia.

シン：今度、一緒に、秋葉原に行きましょう。

R　Shin：Kondo, isshoni, akihabara-ni ikimashou.

Shin：Someday, let's go to Akihabara together!

マイ：約束ですよ。忘れないでくださいね。

R　Mai：Yakusoku-desu-yo. Wasure-na'ide-kudasa'i-ne.

Mai：It's a promise. Please don't forget it!

Let's try! Let's practice! Let's talk in Japanese! ▶ 日本語で会話してみよう！

Challenge & Practice

Let's have a conversation with Miku by choosing a word from Option A to fill [A], and a word from Option B to fill [B] respectively.

N ミク：どこからきたの？
あなた：[A] の [B] から。

R Miku : Doko-kara kita-no?
Anata : [A] no [B] kara.

E Miku : Where are you from?
You : (I'm) from B in A.

	N	R	E
Options [A]	インドネシア アメリカ カナダ フランス イギリス	indoneshia amerika kanada furansu igirisu	Indonesia US Canada France UK

	N	R	E
Options [B]	ジャカルタ ニューヨーク トロント パリ ロンドン	Jakaruta nyûyōku toronto pari rondon	Jakarta NY Toronto Paris London

Model Answer
(1) [A] インドネシア　[B] ジャカルタ
(2) [A] アメリカ　[B] ニューヨーク
(3) [A] カナダ　[B] トロント
(4) [A] フランス　[B] パリ
(5) [A] イギリス　[B] ロンドン

10
巡り、夏
Meguri,natsu

Meguri, natsu ▶ 巡り、夏

Meguri,natsu 巡り、夏

This song contains many words from Japanese summer traditions, such as festivals, enjoyed by children and adults alike. Sing to learn the vocabulary as well as the Japanese sense of the seasons, which go round ("meguru") like a wheel.

▶♪Japanese 日本語

作詞 teaeye
作曲 teaeye
唄 初音ミク

おはよう　おやすみ

繰り返して　進んでく

季節も巡って

暑い夏が　始まる

提灯　あたりを照らし出し ■

わたあめ　桃色になる ■

お囃子　音が近づく ■

リズムに合わせ　心踊る

Look at page 184.

ふわふわ　リボンのへこ帯

揺れる気持ち　うつしてる

しゃくやくの浴衣　ふわり ■

君の顔を　覗き込む

Introduction ▶曲紹介

This song was produced by "teaeye" (pronounced like /tee-eye/) for this book. He is a music producer for VOCALOID, specialised in EDM and technopop. He's been popular since his debut in 2012 at NicoNico Video, and received the Crypton Future Media Award for "New World" at the Sonoca Recording Contest in 2015. This song describes a typical Japanese summer festival, its fireworks, its distinctive seasonality, along with a glimpse of fresh love.

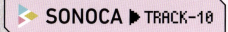

お祭り みんなの
賑やかな雰囲気で
笑顔が溢れて
距離が少し埋まった

人混みに紛れ
はぐれてしまわないように
とっさに握った
手を忘れない この一瞬

見上げる 目線の先に
一筋の光 黒い空に
ヒュルルと火の粉を散らし
期待を上げる 銀笛

Japanese ▶

打ち上がる花火が
夜の空を彩る
残った煙が
余韻残し消えてく

やりたいことが
あれもこれもあるけど
時間は止まらない
終わらないで　この季節

桜が舞い踊り散る　春は
花火が夜空を焦がす　夏は
山や街を赤く染めてく　秋は
雪降る　冬は
全て儚くて

Introduction ▶ 曲紹介

▶ 巡り、頁

落ち葉の絨毯が
この場所に広がっても
重ねる　季節を
君と一緒に　いれたら

おはよう　おやすみ
繰り返して　進んでく
四つの色巡り
物語も　進んでく

Illustration by ポルポネ
© Crypton Future Media, INC. www.piapro.net piapro

Roma-ji

▶ Roma-ji [ローマ字]

Sakushi teaeye
Sakkyoku teaeye
Uta Hatsune Miku

Ohayô, oyasumi

Kurikaeshi-te susun-deku

Kisetsu-mo megu-tte

Atsui natsu-ga hajimaru

Chôchin atari-o terashi-dashi

Wata-ame momo-iro-ni naru

O-hayashi oto-ga chikazuku

Rizumu-ni awase kokoro odoru

Fuwafuwa ribon-no heko obi

Yureru kimochi utsushi-teru

Shakuyaku-no yukata fuwari

Kimi-no kao-o nozoki-komu

Introduction ▶ 曲紹介

▶ Meguri, natsu

O-matsuri min'nano

Nigiyaka-na fun'iki-de

Egao-ga afure-te

Kyori-ga sukoshi uma-tta

Hitogomi-ni magire

Hagure-te shimawa-nai-yôni

Tossa-ni nigi-tta

Te-o wasure-nai kono isshun

Miageru mesen-no saki-ni

Hitosuji-no hikari kuroi sora-ni

Hyururu-to hinoko-o chirashi

Kitai-o ageru ginbué

Meguri, natsu ▶巡り、夏

Roma-ji ▶

Uchi-agaru hanabi-ga

Yoru-no sora-o irodoru

Noko-tta kemuri-ga

Yoin nokoshi ki'e-teku

Yari-tai koto-ga

Are-mo kore-mo aru kedo

Jikan-wa tomara-na'i

Owara-nai-de kono kisetsu

Sakura-ga mai-odori chiru haru-wa

Hanabi-ga yozora-o kogasu natsu-wa

Yama-ya machi-o akaku some-teku aki-wa

Yuki furu fuyu-wa

Subete hakanaku-te

Introduction ▶ 曲紹介

▶ Meguri,natsu

Ochiba-no jûtan-ga

Kono basho-ni hiroga-tte-mo

Kasaneru kisetsu-o

Kimi-to issho-ni ire-tara

Ohayô oyasumi

Kurikaeshi-te susun-deku

Yottsu-no iro meguri

Monogatari-mo susun-deku

Illustration by ボルボネ
© Crypton Future Media, INC. www.piapro.net piapro

179

Meguri, natsu ▶巡り、夏

Translation ▶

▶ Translation 　［ 英訳 ］

Words ▎teaeye
Music ▎teaeye
Vocal ▎Hatsune Miku

Morning, G'night

Continuously repeating

The seasons turn and

Sultry summer begins

The chochin lantern lights the area with a pink cotton candy glow

The sound of the matsuri approaches, our hearts dance with the rhythms

The fluffy ribbon (heko-obi)

reflects my light heart and makes me faint

I softly gaze your face through the peony-floating yukata

Introduction ▶ 曲紹介

▶ Meguri,natsu

The lively matsuri overflows with smiles and good cheer
shortening the distance between us

So we don't get separated in the crowd,
I hold your hand automatically
I will never forget this moment

Looking up, I see a ray of light streaking across the dark sky
A silver whistle, shrieking, sparkling, raising our hopes

Meguri, natsu ▶巡り、夏

Translation ▶

Fireworks far above

colour the night sky,

Their smoking remains

disappearing into a trail

There are so many things

I want to do, but

time never stops its march

I wish this season would never end

Cherry Blossoms fluttering down in spring

Fireworks scorch the sky in summer

Mountains and towns are coloured in red in autumn

Snow falls in winter

All so transient...

Introduction ▶ 曲紹介

▶ Meguri,natsu

Even as autumn covers this place with a carpet of fallen leaves,
The seasons mount, I want to spend them with you

Morning G'night.
Continuously repeating
The seasons turn and four colours revolve our story continues

Illustration by ポルポネ
© Crypton Future Media, INC. www.piapro.net

Meguri, natsu ▶巡り、夏

▶ Context and Japanese Culture

文脈と日本の文化

Bunmyaku to Nihon no Bunka

The Japanese love festivals, events, and celebration. Summer is the season for "matsuri" (祭り：festivals) often derived from memorials of ancestors.

日本のお祭りのことば (word of festivals in Japan)

●提灯　Chôchin are Japanese paper lanterns made with a bamboo frame and paper. They used to sybolize the repose of souls, but now they are a decoration at festivals as well as the doors of "izaka-ya (Japanese casual pubs)".

●わたあめ　Wata-ame is cotton candy. There are many food stalls and children's favourite is wata-ame.

●お囃子　O-hayashi is Japanese Traditional Music for Festivals. you can hear some sounds in the beginning of this song.

●浴衣　Yukata is a casual kimono-like garment which was worn as a bathrobe, but then started to be worn during the summer. Children and young girls often use heko-obi (soft and fluffy sash) as a belt of yukata. These days yukata are very popular among young girls for dressing up for summer events like firework shows (hanabi) and festivals (matsuri).

Context and Japanese Culture ▶ 文脈と日本の文化

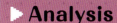
Analysis

Words of festivals in Japan

These are words related with Japanese festivals (matsuri). Matsuri were originally offerings to Shinto deities, but now the word is used for any festival. Matsuri are often held in summer, when it was believed that the restless souls of the dead were comforted.

提灯（**R** chôchin）、わたあめ（**R** wata-ame）、お囃子（**R** o-hayashi）、兵児帯（**R** heko-obi）、浴衣（**R** yukata）、お祭り（**R** o-matsuri）

Key words ヒュルル／ふわふわ

Many Japanese expressions are ideophones, based on sensory perceptions such as sound, feeling, smell, color, shape or movement. In this song, Miku sings ふわふわ (fuwa-fuwa) which conveys the sense of soft touch, ふわり (fuwari, often used as "fuwari-to" as an adverb) means softly. ヒュルルと (hyururu-to) describes the whistling sound when a firework rises in the sky.

Tips 全て儚くて (Subete hakanaku-te)

Everything is transient.
Hakanai (儚い) is an adjective which is used to describe being fleeting; transient; short-lived; momentary; ephemeral; fickle; vain or empty. This word and its concept appear also in early Japanese culture. Not wanting the season to end "Owara-nai-de kono kisetsu" is contrasted with this sense of "hakanasa" (fleeting-ness).

Meguri, natsu ▶巡り、夏

▶ Let's try! Let's practice! Let's talk in Japanese!

日本語で会話してみよう！

Nihongo de kaiwa shitemiyô!

In this song, you hear Miku is counting colours as "yottsu-no iro" or four colours, implying four seasons. Let's learn the basic of counting in Japanese even though there are variety of counting ways in Japanese language.

▶ 基本構文

① 数え方／数詞 how to count

| 1 - hito-tsu | 2 - futa-tsu | 3 - mi-ttsu | 4 - yo-ttsu | 5 - itsu-tsu |
| 6 - mu-ttsu | 7 - nana-tsu | 8 - ya-ttsu | 9 - kokono-tsu | 10 - tô |

The most common counting suffix is "tsu". You can hear it in the last verse of this song, when the colours which represent seasons are counted.
"Tsu" is added to the basic number, and pronounced as the above.
No "tsu" form for over eleven.
This is used to order dishes at restaurant. Useful to learn!

For example,
when we count dogs and cats, we use "hiki" which changes euphonically like:
1匹の犬 i-ppiki no inu (a dog/one dog)
2匹の犬 ni-hiki no inu (two dogs)
3匹の犬 san-biki no inu (three dogs)

Let's try! Let's practice! Let's talk in Japanese! ▶日本語で会話してみよう！

▶ Casual scene SONOCA ▶ TRACK-27

ミク：これ、なあに？
R Miku: Kore na'ani?

Miku：What's this?

きみ：これは、わたあめだよ。
R Kimi: Kore-wa wata-ame-dayo.

You：It's (they are) cotton candy.

ミク：ちょうだい？
R Miku: Chôdai?

Miku：Can I have it?

きみ：いくつ？
R Kimi: Ikutsu?

You：How many?

ミク：3つ、ちょうだい。
R Miku: Mittsu chôdai?

Miku：Three.

きみ：いいよ。
R Kimi: Îyo.

You：Ok.

▶Formal scene　　　SONOCA ▶ TRACK-28

シン：これはなんですか？
R Shin: Kore-wa nan-desu-ka?

マイ：これは、わたあめです。
R Mai: Kore-wa wata-ame-desu.

シン：これをください。
R Shin: Kore-o kudasai.

マイ：いくつですか？
R Mai: Ikutsu-desu-ka?

シン：3つです。
R Shin: Mittsu desu.

マイ：わかりました。
R Mai: Wakarimashita.

Shin : What's this?

Mai : It's (they are) cotton candy.

Shin : Could I have some?

Mai : How many would you like?

Shin : Three.

Mai : Certainly.

Let's try! Let's practice! Let's talk in Japanese! ▶日本語で会話してみよう！

Challenge & Practice

Let's practice how to order at a shop by choosing a word from Option A to fill [A], and a word from Option B to fill [B] respectively.

Example

N　すみません、[A: わたあめ] [B: 3つ] ください。
R　Sumimasen, [A: wata-ame] [B: mittu] kudasai.
E　Excuse me, three cotton candies, please.

N	すみません、	[　　A　　]	[　　B　　] ください。
R	sumimasen,	[　　A　　]	[　　B　　] kudasai.
E	Excuse me,	[　　A　　]	[　　B　　] ,please.
M	Excuse me, [　　B　　][　　A　　], please.		

OptionsA

N	R	E
コーヒー	Kôhî	coffee
ケーキ	kêki	cake
これ	kore	this

OptionsB

N	R	E
1つ	hitotsu	1 (pieces)
2つ	futatsu	2 (pieces)
3つ	mittsu	3 (pieces)

Model Answer
(1) [A] コーヒー　[B] 1つ（1杯）
(2) [A] ケーキ　[B] 2つ
(3) [A] これ　[B] 3つ

Simple Grammar Rules & Pronunciation Guide for Japanese ▶日本語シンプル文法＆発音ガイド

▶ Simple Grammar Rules & Pronunciation

Simple Grammar Rules for Japanese

	Explanation	Example (English)	Example (Japanese)
1	Word order is different from English.	I love you.	私は　あなたを　愛してる。 (I)　　(you)　　(love)
2	Word order is flexible.	I love you.	私は　あなたを　愛してる。 あなたを　私は　愛してる。 Particles differentiate the subject/object.
3	Subjects are often omitted.	I love you.	あなたを愛してる。
4	There are various informal and formal ways.	I love you.	[casual1] あなたを愛しているの。 [casual2] 君を愛してる。 [formal] あなたを愛しています。

190

Guide for Japanese

Simple Pronunciation Guide for Japanese

1	Basically all consonants are followed by vowel.	taberu **E** eat	suki **E** like	suru **E** do
2	Basic vowels are five	a, i, u, e, o		
3	Basic consonants are	k,s,t,n,h, m,y,r,w	not voiced sounds	→ Look at the page "50 Hiragana List" & "50 Katakana List".
		g,z,d,b,p	voiced sounds	

191

Verb & Adjective Conjugation ▶動詞＆形容詞活用表

▶ Verb & Adjective Conjugation

Verb Conjugation

Conjugation	Verb	English	dictionary form
Group 1	歌う	sing	utau
Group 2	食べる	eat	taberu
	見る	look	miru
Group 3	来る	come	kuru
	する	do	suru

Adjective Conjugation

Conjugation	Verb	English	dictionary form
i-Adj.	おもしろい	interesting/funny	omoshiroi
	うつくしい	beautiful	utsukushî
na-Adj.	しずかな	quiet	shizuka(da)
	すき	fond	suki(da)

masu-form(polite)	te-form(connective)	nai-form(denial)
utai-masu	uta-tte	utawa-nai
tabe-masu	tabe-te	tabe-nai
mi-masu	mi-te	mi-nai
ki-masu	ki-te	ko-nai
shi-masu	shi-te	shi-nai

te-form(conjunctive)	nai-form(denial)	ta-form(past)
omoshiroku-te	omoshiroku-nai	omoshirokat-ta
utsukushiku-te	utsukushiku-nai	utsukushikat-ta
shizuka-de	shizuka-ja-nai	shizuka-dat-ta
suki-de	suki-ja-nai	suki-dat-ta

50 Hiragana Lists ▶ ひらがな 50 音表

▶ 50 Hiragana Lists

Here's a list of 50 hiragana in Japanese.
You can learn stroke order in the following list.

50 Katakana Lists

**Here's a list of 50 Katakana in Japanese.
You can learn stroke order in the following list.**

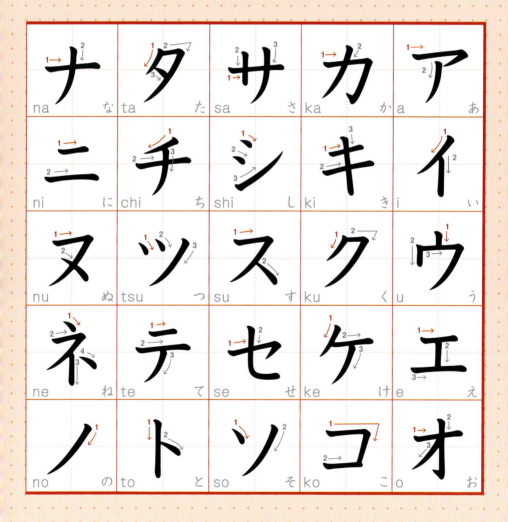

Noricco Akiho-Toyoda

豊田典子
とよだのりこ

▶ **Academic Background**

Noricco Akiho-Toyoda, MA, Applied Linguistics, studied Japanese historical linguistics and second language acquisition in Tokyo and London.

Born in Tokyo as a native Japanese speaker she started speaking English and programming for fun when she was little. Languages, whether human or artificial, have fascinated her ever since. Now being multi-lingual-Japanese, English, French as well as conversational Mandarin and Indonesian, her linguistic talent also covers VBA, Prolog, and coding education.

photo by Junko Yamanaka
やまなか順子・

▶ **Japanese Language & Charity Activities**

She is a keen volunteer in charity and community activities, working with immigrant children in Japan and victim support at the Crown court in London. Noricco is also a consultant, adviser and interpreter for international organizations and Japan's Ministry of Foreign Affairs.

▶ **Love & Otaku**

Growning up in the golden age of Japanese manga and anime, she naturally got fond of listening to Hatsune Miku when she first appeared as a novel VOCALOID. Noricco is so glad to have this opportunity to combine her enthusiasms to both Japanese language and Hatsune Miku.

▶ **Affiliations**

Senior Researcher at S&N Information Limited
Lecturer, Hosei University in Tokyo
Lecturer, Tokyo Kasei University in Tokyo
Lecturer, Meikai University Dentistry School, Japan
Representative, University of London Alumni associations of Japan
Honorary Advisor, Da-Hai Group for Chinese War Orphans
Member of Asia TEFL
Member of The Japan Society for Medical English Education (JASMEE)
Former advisor of IOM, International Organization for Migration

▶ **Publications**

French Phrases 1000, Kokusaigogakusha, Japan
English conversation in 5 min. Sanshusha, Japan
French conversation and pronunciation

クレジット一覧

Illustration by KEI
© Crypton Future Media, INC. www.piapro.net piapro

Illustration by KEI
© Crypton Future Media, INC. www.piapro.net piapro

Licensed by TOY'S FACTORY INC.

「VOCALOID（ボーカロイド）」および「ボカロ」はヤマハ株式会社の商標登録です。
VOCALOID and VOCALO are trademarks of Yamaha Corporation.
http://www.vocaloid.com/

JASRAC 出 1804539-801

添付のSONOCAダウンロード期限：2023年6月30日
This SONOCA CARD is valid until June 30, 2023.

編集協力	デイビッド・ピンスカー
	小俣元、石川悠太 (スタジオ・ハードデラックス)
装丁・本文デザイン・DTP	松本優典、汐田彩貴、下鳥怜奈 (スタジオ・ハードデラックス)

© Crypton Future Media, INC. www.piapro.net **piapro**

初音ミクで日本語
Miku dé Nihongo
～Sing with Hatsune Miku and Learn
　Japanese Culture & Conversation! ～

2018年5月30日　第1刷発行

監　修	クリプトン・フューチャー・メディア株式会社
著　者	豊田典子 (Noricco Toyoda)
発行者	前田俊秀
発行所	株式会社 三修社
	〒150-0001　東京都渋谷区神宮前2-2-22
	TEL03-3405-4511 FAX03-3405-4522
	http://www.sanshusha.co.jp
編集担当	竹内正明・本多真佑子
印刷・製本	日経印刷株式会社

©2018 Noricco Toyoda Printed in Japan
ISBN 978-4-384-05892-5 C2081

JCOPY ＜出版者著作権管理機構 委託出版物＞

本書の無断複製は著作権法上での例外を除き禁じられています。複製される場合は、
そのつど事前に、出版者著作権管理機構 (電話 03-3513-6969 FAX 03-3513-6979
e-mail: info@jcopy.or.jp) の許諾を得てください。